FRAUD IN ACCOUNTS PAYABLE: HOW TO PREVENT IT

FRAUD IN ACCOUNTS PAYABLE: HOW TO PREVENT IT

MARY S. SCHAEFFER

WILEY

JOHN WILEY & SONS, INC.

Published by John Wiley & Sons, Inc., Hoboken, New Jersey.
Published simultaneously in Canada.

For general information on our other products and services, or technical support, please contact our Customer Care Department within the United States at 800-762-2974, outside the United States at 317-572-3993 or fax 317-572-4002.

Wiley also publishes its books in a variety of electronic formats. Some content that appears in print may not be available in electronic books.

For more information about Wiley products, visit our Web site at http://*www.wiley.com*.

Library of Congress Cataloging-in-Publication Data:

Schaeffer, Mary S.
    Fraud in accounts payable: how to prevent it / Mary S. Schaeffer.
        p.   cm.
    Includes index.
    ISBN 978-0-470-26045-6 (cloth)
    1. Accounts payable–Auditing.   2. Auditing, Internal.   I. Title.
    HF5681.A27S36 2008
    657′.74–dc22

2008011985

Printed in the United States of America

10 9 8 7 6 5 4 3 2 1

Books by Mary S. Schaeffer:

Accounts Payable and Sarbanes-Oxley: Strengthening Your Internal Controls (2006)
Accounts Payable Best Practices (2004)
Accounts Payable: A Guide to Running an Efficient Department (2004)
Controller and CFO's Guide to Accounts Payable (2006)
Essentials of Accounts Payable (2002)
Essentials of Credit, Collections, and Accounts Receivable (2002)
International Credit and Collections: A Guide to Extending Credit Worldwide (2001)
New Payment World: A Manager's Guide to Creating an Efficient Payment Process (2007)
Travel & Entertainment Best Practices (2007)

For my anchors
My husband, Hal Schaeffer, and my two children, Ben
and Lara Ludwig

Contents

PREFACE

Fraud and murder have a lot in common. If you've seen even a few detective shows or movies, you know there are three factors for identifying the murderer: means, motive, and opportunity. Alas, the same is true for fraud. And, while we can do very little about motive, this book will provide you with ample tools to clamp down on the means and opportunity. Anytime you have weak internal controls or inappropriate (or nonexistent) segregation of duties, you have provided the opportunity as well as the means.

I recently was reviewing a client's accounts payable operations and the director commented that I saw fraud every place I looked. She was only partially correct. What I saw was the opportunity for fraud. And unfortunately for organizations everywhere, employees are best positioned to uncover those hidden pockets of weaknesses where the organization is vulnerable. This book will help you do just that.

It is probably important to point out that it is impossible to completely stop fraud; or should I say stop crooks from trying to steal from you? However, you can make it extremely difficult for them—so difficult that they give up and take their efforts elsewhere. That is half of the goal of this book: to provide tactics and strategies so that fraudsters will take their business elsewhere. Yet, we have to be realistic. From time to time, fraud will occur. The other goal of the book is to provide you with the tools to help you detect fraud, should it occur on your watch.

There is a side benefit from installing best practices to deter fraud, and it is a big one. Many of the strategies and tactics used to deter crime will also deter duplicate payments. So, by instituting some of the practices we'll discuss in the book, you will at the same time be improving your accounts payable operations and taking a whack at the duplicate payment issue, which virtually every organization has.

As we'll discuss in detail in the chapters of this book, an organization's greatest vulnerability is not from the new employee, the one who is given little access, but rather from the long-term, trusted employee. This is, unfortunately, who commits the lion's share of insider fraud. In fact, many of the chapters have a section at the end called "Fraud in the Real World." There are over 50 tales throughout the book that come mostly from readers of *Accounts Payable Now & Tomorrow*, although a few came from the newspapers and from some of my colleagues.

As you will see as you read through them, we are all vulnerable. No organization can afford to take the issue of fraud lightly. The stories demonstrate the lengths to which employees will sometimes go in order to steal from their employers. Reading through the stories, I could only think, "I couldn't have made some of this stuff up if I tried."

As I was writing this book, the fraud at French banking giant Société Générale unfolded. It is alleged that the trader used his knowledge of the group's security systems to conceal fraudulent trading positions. It was the fellow's intricate knowledge of the control system of every aspect of trading at the bank that allowed him to build up fraudulent positions and hide them. Unbelievably, it is alleged that he played around with spreadsheets as well. The story demonstrates, I believe, that organizations are at risk from both outside and within.

The book starts with an in-depth analysis of just exactly who commits fraud. When *Accounts Payable Now & Tomorrow* conducted its fraud survey, one of the respondents indicated she would like to know if the risk was from internal or external sources. By the end of this chapter, you will realize that, alas, the risk is on both fronts.

The book then dives into the problem of check fraud. It continues to plague payment professionals everywhere. And it seems like the moment the banking community comes up with a product to thwart the thieves, the crooks find another way to get their hands on money that doesn't belong to them. The chapter on check fraud, as I had initially written it, was so long that the information was separated into two chapters, with a separate chapter devoted to the issue of check stock. No matter how much we'd all love to get away from paper, it looks like we will be stuck with some for the foreseeable future. Even after dividing the information into two sections, there is a ton of information on check fraud.

The book then turns to look at other payment mechanisms, namely, p-card and electronic payments, and provides some advice on preventing and detecting fraud in these two arenas. I'm happy to report, at least at this point, that fraud in these two areas is not a huge issue. I can only hope it stays that way. And the best way to ensure that it doesn't become an issue for you is to make sure you have the right controls in place. These are discussed in Chapters 4 and 5.

We then turn our microscope to the issue of travel and entertainment fraud. You will not believe some of the stories contained in that chapter. You can't make this stuff up. The chapter offers best practices and suggestions on fraud prevention in the T&E arena.

Although I fervently believe petty cash boxes should not be part of the business payment landscape and recommend such, we still have some advice for those who continue to be saddled with petty cash.

Vendors are not all honest and, in fact, some of them are downright dishonest. We've got a look at some of the common scams, as well as bad practices to avoid in the vendor arena. Related to the issue of invoice fraud is the subject of master vendor files. Many don't realize that by not incorporating proper practices with regard to the master vendor file, they are opening the door to employee fraud. We explain exactly how this works and what you should do to ensure that this does not occur on your watch.

Before the first part of the book closes, we investigate payroll fraud and telecom fraud, with a ream of recommendations that will help you prevent these frauds. The stuff on telecom fraud is mind-blowing, and we have an expert who shares his insights on what every organization should do so that this insidious fraud does not happen to them.

After going through the different types of accounts payable fraud, the book shifts focus slightly and looks at the issue as one mass rather than focusing on individual types. We look at really bad practices in accounts payable that allow all sorts of frauds to flourish. I hope when you see the fraud some of these common practices permit, you will eliminate them from your accepted practices.

We've got a rather long look at the types of reports you can and should run to help determine if fraud has occurred. Ideally, you will find nothing, but if you have fraud, these reports should point you in the right direction. We close with some advice that will help any organization in its fraud detection and prevention program. We call these tactics for the Average Joe or Jane because they require no investment of money; they are something any organization with the right mind-set can do.

Having read this far, I invite you to open the book and take the fraud detection and prevention journey. I wish you the best of luck.

Crooks are quite inventive. Although I have covered every possible type of fraud related to accounts payable, I can guarantee that when it is time to update this book, there will be frauds not covered in this book. In fact, I may have missed one or two this time around, although I hope I got everything. I invite readers who discover a different fraud or a story not covered in this book to contact me with that information. It is very much appreciated. Send your information to either mary@maryschaeffer.com or marys@ap-now.com and accept my gratitude in advance.

If I have either frightened you or at least made you think about your organization's vulnerability to fraud, I have succeeded. Every organization is vulnerable and needs to take the appropriate steps to both detect and prevent fraud. Fraud insidiously eats away at your bottom line, and hits to the bottom line are something few organizations can afford. I wish you the best of luck in protecting your organization.

September 2008

ACKNOWLEDGMENTS

I could not have undertaken this exploration of fraud without the help of many individuals: readers who readily and honestly shared their stories of real-life frauds, and the experts, Bob Lovallo of Pinpoint Profit Recovery and Mark Evans of BottaBoom Consulting LLC, who willingly shared both their expertise and stories. You all make this book come alive by providing me with real-life examples that give new meaning to the saying, "Truth is stranger than fiction," or as I like to say, "You can't make this stuff up."

I had wanted to write a book about fraud for some time but had not done so. About a year ago, I was invited by Bob Cohen (thanks, Bob) to give several talks for Basware. He asked for suggested topics, and when I suggested fraud, they agreed. When we saw the turnout, I knew the time had come for this book and, thankfully, Sheck Cho and John Wiley agreed. A special big thanks has to go to Sheck for being such a supportive editor and advocate for my books.

PART ONE

WHERE ACCOUNTS PAYABLE FRAUD CAN HAPPEN IN YOUR ORGANIZATION

As you will see as you work your way through the first portion of this book, crooks looking to get money from your firm can be pretty darn creative. When most people think of accounts payable fraud, or payment fraud, their minds usually focus on check fraud. And that is with good reason. Check fraud is a huge issue in this country. In fact, it was referred to as one of the biggest growth industries in the early 1990s.

But we've come a long way, and there are now many deterrents that make check fraud more difficult. However, at the same time, advances in technology have put the tools to commit check fraud within the financial reach of virtually anyone who wants to commit it. It is a constant battle, with the crooks trying to get their grimy hands on your money and the banks and software developers introducing new products to thwart those fraudsters. The battle is interesting and continually changing.

At the same time, if we focus solely on check fraud, we are looking at only a portion of the fraud picture when it comes to accounts payable–related functions. Fraudsters know they can play a variety of other games taking advantage of payroll, petty cash, your master vendor file, your employees' desktops, your credit cards, automated clearinghouse (ACH), and the invoices your legitimate and phony vendors send you.

So, as you can see, there is still a lot to cover even after we finish with the check stuff. While check fraud may be a big tip of the iceberg, there are still lots of other ways for crooks to get your money. In this Part, we'll dissect them all.

1

PROFILES OF FRAUD IN THE BUSINESS WORLD

In responding to an *Accounts Payable Now & Tomorrow* Fraud Survey, one savvy professional wrote, "I hope to find out if fraud is generally internal or external to an organization. Can we trust our employees? Or is it someone from the outside that we need to be wary of?" She brings up a very good point. Where should executives focus their resources when it comes to protecting their organization from fraud? By the end of this chapter, you will have the answer to this question.

Without a doubt, everyone reading this is at some risk for employee fraud, also referred to as occupational fraud. When you think about it, the explanation is simple. Who better than your employees know where the weaknesses are in your processes? And even if your processes are iron tight, your employees will know how to get around the controls you've worked so hard to put in place. Now, some reading this may be scratching their heads, thinking I'm making a mountain out of a molehill. Before we dive into the statistics that demonstrate just how common fraud is in the corporate world, let's look at some of the myths that surround fraud in the corporate world.

THREE BIG MYTHS

When it comes to fraud, there are a number of misconceptions. The three biggies are:

1. It could never happen here.
2. My employees would never steal from me.
3. We have good segregation of duties, except for a few long-time, trusted employees who would never steal from us.

As you will see after reading this chapter, all three are false. It could happen in your shop and, in fact, has in almost every organization; sadly, a few of your employees will steal from you given the opportunity; and saddest of all, if an employee does steal from you, the odds are high that it will be one of your long-term, trusted employees.

FRAUD STATISTICS

Generally speaking, reported fraud statistics understate the problem. The reason is twofold:

1. People can report only what has been discovered. Undetected fraud can never be included in the statistics.

2. People are sometimes embarrassed to admit they have been the victim of fraud, especially when it demonstrates a shortcoming on their part. However, given the numbers you are about to see, it is not clear that this is still as strong a factor as it once was.

Throughout this book, you'll see reference to three sources of statistics. They all have different target audiences, yet they all tell a similar, chilling story. The sources are:

1. The Association of Certified Fraud Examiners' (ACFE's) *Report to the Nation*
2. PricewaterhouseCoopers (PwC) Global Economic Survey
3. *Accounts Payable Now & Tomorrow*'s (APN&T's) Fraud Survey

We should also point out that the surveys do not ask the same questions, but, again, the conclusions that can be drawn from the numbers are similar. PwC asked its survey respondents about "significant" crime. It was left to the respondent to decide what was significant and what wasn't. In this case, over 43 percent responded that their organization had suffered one or more significant economic crimes within the prior two years.

The APN&T respondents were asked if any organization the respondent had worked for in the past ten years had been a victim of any sort of fraud. In that instance, a whopping 86 percent responded affirmatively.

While the time frames are clearly different and the questions are not identical, the conclusion cannot be denied. Every organization must be concerned about fraud and take the necessary steps to guard against it.

In providing commentary to the APN&T survey, one of the respondents questioned whether the threat to her organization was internal or external. As the rest of the numbers will illustrate, the threat is dual. No organization can afford to let its guard down on either front.

OCCUPATIONAL FRAUD: IT'S A *BIG* PROBLEM

Occupational fraud is just as ugly as it sounds. Every two years, in a widely awaited *"Report to the Nation,"* the ACFE provides an update on this topic. The 2006 report contains some fascinating information that is especially relevant to those concerned about accounts payable (AP). Why? Because it examines three of the most common frauds related to AP:

1. Check tampering
2. Billing schemes
3. Expense reimbursements

DEFINITIONS AND FREQUENCY

The ACFE describes occupational fraud as "the use of one's occupation for personal enrichment through the deliberate misuse or misapplication of the employing organization's resources or assets." Of those cases reported, 91.5 percent involve asset misappropriations, with a median loss of $150,000.

Billing schemes, the most common, are described as "any scheme in which a person causes his or her employer to issue a payment by submitting invoices for fictitious goods or services, inflated invoices, or invoices for personal purchases." This can be done by the employee's creating a shell company and billing the employer for nonexistent services or the employee's submitting invoices for personal items. A whopping 28.3 percent of the cases of misappropriated assets were of this type, and the median loss was a mind-boggling $130,000.

Check tampering is defined as "any scheme in which a person steals his or her employer's funds by forging or altering a check on one of the organization's bank accounts, or steals a check the organization has legitimately issued to another payee." This can be done by the employee's either stealing a blank company check or taking a check made out to a vendor and depositing it into his or her own bank account. A little over 17 percent of the asset misappropriation frauds were related to check tampering, with a median loss of $120,000 associated with this type of fraud.

And then there is expense reimbursement fraud, defined as "any scheme in which an employee makes a claim for reimbursement of fictitious or inflated business expenses." Readers of this book have probably seen more than their share of this type of fraud, which accounts for 19.5 percent of asset misappropriations. The median loss related to expense reimbursement fraud is $25,000.

WHO GETS HIT THE HARDEST?

Regrettably, small businesses continue to suffer a disproportionate share of fraud losses. The median loss suffered by organizations with fewer than 100 employees was $190,000 per scheme. This was higher than the median loss in even the largest organizations.

The most common occupational frauds in small businesses involve employees fraudulently writing company checks, skimming revenues, and processing fraudulent invoices.

HOW FRAUD IS DETECTED

As much as I would like to report that internal processes uncover most fraud, that is just not the case. By far, the largest number of cases is discovered because of a tip, and the second-largest number #3 comes to light by accident. Here is a rundown of how frauds are initially discovered:

Tips	34.9%
By accident	25.4
Internal audit	20.2
Internal controls	19.2
External audit	12.0
Notified by police	3.8

(If you do the math, you will note that occasionally two methods are credited for the discovery.)

What this demonstrates is that organizations are not doing a good job at either preventing or detecting fraud. What is truly disheartening is the fact that over half the frauds are detected through methods that have nothing to do with the controls put in place by the organization. In fact, the tips often come about because the crook couldn't keep his or her big mouth shut and bragged about their "accomplishments," resulting in the tip. It is also why anonymous hotlines are such an important component in discovering fraud.

WHO COMMITS OCCUPATIONAL FRAUD?

According to the ACFE, long-term, trusted employees continue to have a stranglehold on this type of crime. Larger losses are associated with employees in higher positions as well as those who have been employed for a longer time. There is a direct correlation between the size of the loss and these two factors.

Men are over one-and-a-half times more likely than women to commit this type of fraud, and when they do, the losses are two-and-a-half times as large. Is this tied to the fact that in most organizations men tend to hold higher positions than women?

Since readers of this book are most apt to run into check tampering and expense reimbursement schemes, I thought I would take a look at the biggest perpetrators of each. If you are thinking sales and/or purchasing, think again.

While sales is the third-largest abuser on the expense reimbursement side, they fall far behind executive/upper management, who account for over one-third of all this type of crime, and accounting, who commit just under 32 percent of it. When it comes to check tampering, accounting (probably because of its familiarity with the issues) is responsible for a whopping 57.4 percent of the cases, with executive/upper management responsible for another 26.4 percent of the cases.

TO PROSECUTE OR NOT

While there is lingering reluctance to prosecute offenders, just over 70 percent of the cases included in this study were referred to law enforcement. The median loss in the referred cases was $200,000, about double that of the cases that were not referred. Fear of adverse publicity continues to be the primary reason for not prosecuting. Almost 44 percent indicated that this was their motivation for declining to take legal action.

Another third of the respondents said that they felt internal discipline was sufficient and a slightly lower number indicated that they had come to a private settlement with the perpetrator. A little over 21 percent believed that it would be too costly to take action. This probably accounts for the lower median loss on nonreported cases. The remaining reasons include:

- Lack of evidence
- Civil suit
- Disappearance of the perpetrator

The other reason that organizations may be reluctant to take legal action is that their chances of recovering a reasonable amount of the loss are not very good. Only 16.4 percent recovered 100 percent of their loss, while 42 percent received nothing.

However, it should be noted that a well-publicized prosecution can do wonders for stopping other potential internal thieves, and we are not necessarily talking about the media. Making sure that everyone within the company is aware that legal action was taken should do the trick.

This report is just one of the many resources available from the ACFE (www.acfe.com).

IS FRAUD AN EQUAL OPPORTUNITY CRIME?

Do you have a preconceived notion as to whether fraudsters are more likely to be male or female? This is one area where the numbers do not tell the same story.

According to the ACFE, 61 percent of the frauds were committed by men. However, the PwC data show that 85 percent of the perpetrators were male. This is a bit of a difference. The explanation probably lies in the makeup of the people interviewed. The PwC respondents tended to be very high-level executives who were asked about "significant" crime, while the ACFE respondents were fraud examiners and did not differentiate between frauds where the losses were big and those where it wasn't.

FRAUD IN THE EYES OF THE BEHOLDER

As we sift through the mountains of data related to fraud, one of the issues is the way an organization views fraud, especially if committed by insiders. One organization might consider it a firing offense, another might only give an employee a warning, and still others might ignore it completely.

Thus, if an organization is serious about preventing fraud, it is crucial that the message is sent from the top. In reality, what we observe is that one organization will fire (and possibly even prosecute) an employee for a relatively minor infraction, while another will completely ignore it.

Take the example of two travelers putting in for the same meal, splitting the profit. In most organizations, if this deed were discovered, the employees would be given a reprimand and asked to reimburse the company for the excess charges. In reality, at the organization where this happened, the two employees were fired and given no references. The organization was serious about fraud, and in its eyes, the employees stole from the company—which, technically, they did. However, there is the concept of letting the punishment fit the crime.

Clearly, in the case of petty theft, there are arguments on both sides of the fence regarding the proper action to be taken when it is uncovered.

EFFECT OF STATUS OF FRAUDSTER

Rank does apparently have its privileges when it comes to fraud. The PwC study found that many did not refer fraudsters from the rank of senior management for criminal prosecution. It also noted that there was a significant difference in the way companies dealt with senior managers involved in a fraud as compared with other employees. In fact, the survey pointed out that when it comes to senior management, the corporate response appears to be limited to warnings or reprimands.

While this is clearly not fair, it is a fact of life, at least for the present time. Needless to say, at the organizations where this occurs, the effect on morale is not positive.

BIG BOSS ISSUE

The numbers highlight another issue, especially when it comes to expense reimbursement fraud. Few employees, especially those at lower levels, are likely to feel comfortable questioning an expense report of an executive at the vice president level or higher. Yet, as the numbers above demonstrate, that's where a good portion of certain types of fraud happen.

At the end of Chapter 7, there is a story of an executive's putting in for a pocketbook costing $3,000. The processor was then put in an awkward position: do they question the clearly inappropriate expense and risk the wrath of that employee and possible career damage, or do they say nothing and process the expense report, which has been approved by the traveler's supervisor? Many of the accounts payable processors I have run into would question the charge, and I admire them for their gumption.

The responsibility for this, as will be discussed in greater detail in the chapter on travel and entertainment (Chapter 7), should be with the person who approved the expense report. However, as will also be discussed in greater detail in Chapter 7, most approvers don't look at the report, they merely scribble their signature on it without ever looking at what is included.

By insisting that people review what they are signing and then holding approvers responsible for losses associated with their own careless review, some steps may be taken against the frauds that are perpetrated due to the hasty reviews.

Along this line, you might want to consider giving every employee in the review chain the right to question any expense on a report or invoice.

WHY DO INSIDERS STEAL?

While you may be thinking the reason employees steal from their employers is they need the money, you would be correct only part of the time. PwC analyzed the data and found the following reasons for the theft (you will note that some thefts had multiple reasons; hence, the numbers exceed 100 percent):

Financial incentive (greed!)	57%
Low temptation threshold	44
Lack of awareness of wrongdoing	40
Expensive lifestyle	36
Denial of financial consequences	26
Career disappointment	12
Potential job loss	8

CONDITIONS THAT PERMIT FRAUDS TO OCCUR

PwC also analyzed the data to pinpoint the shortfalls within the organizations that permitted the fraud to occur. As above, they often assigned blame to several issues, and thus the numbers, if added together, will exceed 100 percent. The main reasons were:

Low commitment to the brand	34%
Insufficient controls	34
Ability to override controls	19
Too great staff anonymity	17
High company targets	13
Corporate ethics unclear	14

These are areas you can do something about. Tight internal controls are well within the bounds of what every organization can establish.

The ability to override controls is a serious matter. While there are times it may be required, the approvals needed should go up the chain of command several levels, and there should be regular reporting any time it is done. It should be a rarity used only when no other approach will work. Require documentation and approvals.

WHY AREN'T MORE FRAUDSTERS PROSECUTED?

The answer to this question is simple. The most common reason fraud isn't prosecuted is that the very act of prosecuting makes the fraud public. And this is something that many organizations loathe. They believe the fact that the fraud occurred demonstrates a lack of appropriate controls on their part. And, in many cases they are correct.

In fact, the ACFE figures show that fear of bad publicity is the number one reason why companies decline to prosecute.

FRAUD IN THE REAL WORLD

A husband and wife "team" created two nonexistent corporations, letterhead, and invoices. Post office boxes and bank accounts were opened for the fictitious corporations. The invoices were sent to the husband's place of employment for maintenance supplies. In his position as building and maintenance manager, the husband would approve the invoices for payment. Once the checks arrived, the wife would deposit them and write checks to herself or cash. Before the scam was uncovered, the pair had netted $400,000.

How were they discovered? Not content with the money they were stealing through their ingenious scheme, the husband succumbed to the allure of easy money and began putting personal charges on his corporate account. An audit of the credit card uncovered the fraudulent charges and triggered the larger investigation, which uncovered the ongoing fraud.

This couple had a good thing going. They had avoided some of the more common mistakes employees make when stealing from their employers. However, like many other thieves, they got greedy. It is not clear if their fraud would have ever been uncovered had it not been for the credit card charges.

By the way, the organization where this occurred lacked the appropriate internal controls and segregation of duties that in the normal course of affairs would have prevented this. Use of a purchase order (PO) process and three-way match would have uncovered this fraud early on. While we do not recommend POs for every purchase, purchases of this magnitude should be done under the auspices of a PO process.

The husband pled guilty, but his now ex-wife did not, claiming she was an innocent participant. She was prosecuted and convicted, and at the time of this writing was requesting a new trial and a new lawyer.

CONCLUDING THOUGHTS

By now, you probably realize you are at risk both internally and externally. In fact, the PwC study asked respondents about this issue, and 76 percent of them reported that the crimes were committed by external parties. However, they were asked only about significant frauds. We believe that most travel and entertainment fraud would not be considered significant, and had it been included, the numbers would be more equal. Even if this is not the case, there still appears to be significant risk from insiders.

This is not to say that every employee is out to defraud his or her employer. Just the opposite is true. Probably less than 1 in 1,000 or even 10,000 eyes their employer's coffers as a target for extra income. The problem, as the preceding statistics hopefully demonstrate, is that it is virtually impossible to tell which one of your employees is the potential bad apple. Hence, executives must institute the appropriate internal controls and segregation of duties within their operations so no employee can take advantage—even your long-term, trusted staff.

At the same time, implementing safeguards against fraud from outsiders is crucial. As the rest of the book will demonstrate, no one is exempt. The excuse of "we're too small," or the reverse, "we're too big," holds no water when it comes to thieves. They will take whatever they can from whomever makes it the easiest for them. Your job: to make sure it is difficult to steal from your organization so they set their sights on someone else.

2

CHECK FRAUD: STILL A HUGE PROBLEM

Check fraud has been a growth industry for a long time. Advancements in printing and copying technology have brought the costs down and put the technology in the hands of virtually anyone who wants it. Combine this with the low risk of being caught associated with the crime, at least from the criminals' standpoint, and it's a wonder anyone bothers to hold up convenience stores and the like.

When you combine the low risk of capture with the fact that, even if captured, the odds of going to jail are small, it's a miracle check fraud isn't even more prevalent. What's more, the crooks are getting smarter. Every advance made by the banking community is matched very quickly by the crooks, as they figure out a way to get around the new security. This chapter will start off by looking at the fraud right under your nose: that committed by your own employees.

This issue is so huge that you will find this chapter much longer than all the others. There are just so many topics to cover.

INTERNAL CONTROLS TO PREVENT CHECK FRAUD BY INSIDERS

This is certainly an unpleasant topic. And while we would like to believe that employee fraud is something that happens only at other companies, the numbers tell a different story. Sadly, from time to time, it happens in our own backyard. In fact, due to the seriousness of the issue, a group comprised of representatives from various branches of government has put together some recommendations to help prevent this type of fraud. But before we look at their advice, let's see just how bad the problem is.

Extent of the Problem

In its 2006 "Report to the Nation on Occupational Fraud and Abuse," the Association of Certified Fraud Examiners (ACFE) reported that 17 percent of all schemes involving fraudulent disbursements of cash involved check tampering. It describes this grouping as "any scheme in which a person steals his or her employer's funds by forging or altering a check on one of the organization's bank accounts, or steals a check the organization has legitimately issued to another payee."

The ACFE breaks down this type of activity into two main scenarios:

1. Employee steals blank company checks and makes them out to himself or an accomplice.
2. Employee steals outgoing check to a vendor and deposits it into her own bank account.

The average dollar amount for these frauds is $120,000, so you can see why organizations need to take this issue seriously.

Who Else Is Concerned?

Obviously, banks are concerned about check fraud. But they aren't alone. The federal government has its concerns as well. The Bank Fraud Working Group is composed of regulatory and law enforcement agencies that either regulate financial institutions or investigate fraud committed against them. The group seeks to improve coordination between agencies and regulators in the investigation and prosecution of financial institution fraud. One of its subgroups, the Check Fraud Working Group, is comprised of representatives from the following agencies:

- Federal Bureau of Investigation
- Department of Justice
- Federal Deposit Insurance Corporation
- Federal Reserve Board
- Internal Revenue Service
- Office of the Comptroller of the Currency
- Office of Thrift Supervision
- U.S. Postal Inspection Service
- National Credit Union Administration
- U.S. Secret Service

Clearly, this is an issue of concern.

RECOMMENDED CONTROLS

The following controls are adapted from the Bank Fraud Working Group's recommendations. Specifically, to guard against insider fraud, organizations should:

- Ensure that changes to vendor information, such as adding names or changing addresses and/or other information, are authorized by the vendor and/or someone responsible for the account in writing, or in a way that guarantees the authenticity of the change. This is especially important if the "remit to" address of a supplier or bank account for an electronic payment is changed.
- Maintain permanent signature cards for each person allowed to approve invoices for payment. This should contain their everyday signature and not their Sunday school flourish.
- Segregate duties to ensure that no one person can set up a vendor in the master vendor file, approve an invoice, and/or sign a check.
- Ensure that vendor complaints and discrepancy reconcilements are directed to staff who are separate from the

transaction (i.e., not someone who could sweep it under the rug).

- Conduct thorough and complete background investigations of new hires.
- Establish appropriate procedures for uncashed checks to ensure proper reporting for unclaimed property.

WHAT ELSE CAN YOU DO?

It goes without saying that appropriate care should be taken of check stock and checks from the initiation of the check run through the mail stage. Checks are especially vulnerable during this process. As noted by the ACFE, these are prime "opportunities" for employees determined to steal from their employers. What's more, organizations sometimes are quite lax about checks during the process.

It is not unheard of to find signed checks in someone's desk, in someone's inbox, tucked under the desk where, hopefully, no one will see them, or worse. Even unsigned checks present thieves with a golden opportunity. That's because, as readers are well aware, few banks verify the signatures on checks. Thus, to a crook, a printed unsigned check is almost as good as a signed one.

HOW BAD IS THE CHECK FRAUD PROBLEM?

Once upon a time, when life in accounts payable was certainly simpler, banks routinely absorbed the losses associated with check fraud. But those losses grew to the point where that was no longer feasible or reasonable. In 1990, the Uniform Commercial Code (UCC) was changed and the concepts of ordinary care and comparative negligence were introduced. These concepts are used to determine liability if there is a check fraud. With check fraud continuing to rocket, accounts payable needs to review what they should be doing.

Today, the problem is four times as large as it was in 1993—and remember, that was after the banks had had enough and the UCC was changed. According to figures from the Nilson Report in 2003, check fraud exceeded $20 billion per year. This is a significant increase from the $5 billion figure reported in 1993 and 1996, when it was $12 billion. Looking at these numbers, it's easy to understand why banks are drawing a line in the sand and companies are taking aggressive steps to protect themselves.

Not only has the check fraud problem exploded, but the resulting changes in the UCC have had an unintended consequence. While the goal was to reduce check fraud, the result of the change was to put corporations and their bankers on opposite sides of the table. Let's face it, if there's a loss, someone has to pay for it. And with banks no longer willing to foot the bill, the issue can get ugly.

WHAT DOES THE LAW SAY?

First, there are three parties to be considered when assessing responsibility for a check fraud loss:

1. The party that issued the check (that's your company)
2. The bank where the check was first deposited
3. The collecting bank

The idea is that each party operates in a manner that minimizes the possibility for check fraud. In Articles 3 and 4, the UCC describes the responsibilities needed under the concepts of ordinary care and comparative negligence. Generally speaking, the losses associated with a check fraud are allocated to the parties (listed above) sharing the responsibility for the prevention of the check fraud. The allocation depends on the parties' ability to prevent the fraud. In other words, it depends on the amount of contributory negligence each party is assessed.

The other contributing factor is a concept called *ordinary care*. This requires that customers follow "reasonable commercial standards" for their industry or business. This seemingly innocuous statement can have significant ramifications—so don't overlook it. An organization's failure to exercise ordinary care will be considered to have substantially contributed to the fraud. Or, to put it another way, they are considered to have neglected their obligation to exercise ordinary care.

IMPACT ON ACCOUNTS PAYABLE

So, what exactly is meant by ordinary care when it comes to your disbursement practices? If you are thinking that reasonable care means good, strong internal controls related to your check preparation and storage processes, you are on the right track. But you are only part of the way there. Your banker may consider not using positive pay, not exercising ordinary care. Without a doubt, positive pay is one of the best steps a company can take to stop check fraud in its tracks. Every company should use it, but a significant number of companies still don't.

Some banks are so insistent that their customers use positive pay that they insert a statement in their deposit agreements that effectively places the liability for check fraud on their customers if the customer does not use positive pay. Accounts payable rarely sees the deposit agreements. Typically, the treasurer or controller will handle this document. If they are not sufficiently informed about the positive pay issue, this could slip past them.

You may be wondering if this is legal. The UCC does not permit banks to simply disclaim their responsibility. However, the rules do not prevent parties from agreeing to shift liability from one party to another. And that is what your company has done if it accepts that depository agreement.

WHAT SHOULD YOU DO?

Use positive pay. It is simply the best safeguard your company has against check fraud. Please see the discussion below for an explanation of positive pay and the enhancements that some banks have introduced to make the product stronger.

If your organization is not using positive pay, ask to see the deposit agreement to make sure that bank has not passed the liability to your organization. Claiming ignorance will get you nowhere if a fraudulent check makes it through the system. Even if there is nothing in the deposit agreement, you might inquire from the treasurer, controller, or whoever is responsible for banking relationships if the firm ever signed a letter refusing to accept positive pay. Some banks require this and use it as a defense to shift payment responsibility to their customers in cases of check fraud. We've heard of several cases where the bank refused an account if positive pay wasn't used without a signed letter.

Check fraud is a fact of business life. No matter how careful an organization is, it happens. Virtually every company gets hit at one point or another. By knowing what the risks and alternatives are, you will be in the best position to limit your firm's exposure in case of check fraud.

POSITIVE PAY AND ITS COUSINS

Positive pay is a product banks use to help thwart check fraud. Virtually every check expert agrees that it is the best defense against check fraud. However, crooks are a resourceful lot, and just as quickly as the legitimate business world develops protection against them, the fraudsters find ways to circumvent the safeguards. This has happened to some extent with positive pay and has led to some very interesting innovations as the corporate world protects itself against check fraud.

The Basic Model

The basic positive pay model requires that a company send a file to the bank each time it does a check run. The file contains check numbers and dollar amounts of all checks issued. The bank then matches all checks that come in for clearing against this file. Once a check comes in and is paid, the item is removed from the file and cannot be paid again.

This approach took a big whack at the check fraud problem. It eliminated several huge check fraud issues, including:

- The copying of one check numerous times and the subsequent cashing of all of them
- The altering of the dollar amount on a check
- The complete manufacture of fraudulent checks drawn on an organization's bank account

What the basic model did not address were checks cashed by tellers and checks where the payee's name was changed. Additionally, companies that could not produce a check-issued file for transmission to their banks were left unprotected. And, as might be expected, once the crooks got wind of positive pay, some adjusted their sights, focusing more on changing the payee's name rather than the dollar amount and on checks cashed at teller windows. But before we look at the products that address those issues, let's take a look at the banks' response to those companies that could not produce a check-issued file.

Reverse Positive Pay

Recognizing that not every organization was able or willing to produce the tape needed for positive pay, banks introduced another service. It's called *reverse* because it reverses the process. Each morning, the bank tells the company what checks have been presented for clearing. It is up to the company to check those listings and make sure that they are all legitimate. Typically, there is a fall-back position if the company does not notify the bank, and usually that is that the bank pays on the check. The action should be discussed with the bank when the reverse positive pay relationship is initially set up.

Teller Positive Pay

Once it became obvious that checks were being verified before they were honored, crooks realized that most tellers did not have this information and started cashing phony checks in person. Some banks now make this information available to their tellers on the platforms. If your bank is one such bank, ask how frequently this information is updated. Some update continuously, while others only update this information over night. If it is only overnight, you could have some angry or annoyed vendors or employees on your hands if they try to cash checks you give them on the same day they are issued. A phone call usually takes care of these situations.

Payee Name Positive Pay

Recognizing that fraudsters were reduced to focusing their efforts on changing the payee names on checks, a few banks have taken up the fight in that regard. In addition to the check number and dollar amount, they will also verify the payee name. As time goes on, this will become the accepted model of positive pay for use by every organization. Will this completely stop check fraud? Probably not, but it certainly will make it more difficult for the crooks trying to separate your company from its funds.

INTERNAL CONTROLS, SEGREGATION OF DUTIES, AND POSITIVE PAY EXCEPTIONS

When the bank calls asking about a clearing check that wasn't included on the positive pay file, who handles the call, does the checking, and then tells the bank to pay or not to? On the face of it, this is a simple issue. In some organizations it isn't given a lot of consideration and is just added onto the already overflowing plate in accounts payable. But is this where it really belongs? Does it present a segregation-of-duties issue? The answer depends on the size of the accounts payable department, but in many instances it's a resounding *absolutely!*

The handling of positive pay exception items is frequently done outside the accounts payable department. The most common areas are treasury and the person doing the bank reconciliations.

In a few organizations where the accounts payable department is large enough to have adequate segregation of duties, the handling of exception items is done in accounts payable. It should be noted that in a number of organizations, even though the accounts payable department has an adequate number of employees to take up the issue while maintaining appropriate segregation of duties, the exception handling is still addressed outside accounts payable.

This is an issue all organizations need to address to ensure that appropriate controls and segregation of duties are in place.

INTERNAL CONTROLS AND PAPER CHECKS

Although often overlooked in the overall scheme of the accounts payable world, how checks are handled before, during, and after the print cycle can radically affect an organization in several ways. Before the check gets put in the proverbial mail, there are numerous places where trouble can arise if the paper checks are not handled correctly. Few outside accounts payable realize just how paper and labor intensive the check process can be. And both paper and labor can introduce problems into the process.

WHAT CAN GO WRONG

There is a big debate regarding the use of preprinted check stock versus laser-printed checks. Although preprinted check stock is still in use, a growing number of organizations are moving away from it. For one thing, it increases the risk of fraud if proper controls are not used. Then there is the storage issue. If your check stock is not adequately stored, anyone walking by could filch some stock and write a fraudulent check on your account. If access to the storage location is not limited, control is lost. Proper storage is only the first step to ensuring that check losses are minimized.

Even if you do all this right, you can still be subject to fraud. Anyone who gets your bank account number (and for starters, that's anyone you pay by check), has the necessary information to produce a phony check that will pass muster at most banks, if positive pay is not used.

CONSEQUENCES OF POOR INTERNAL CHECK PRODUCTION PROCESSES

Without other controls in place, fraudulent checks can result in a bottom-line loss. Because the check fraud issue has gotten so bad, the UCC was changed in 1990 to make the party who is in the best position to prevent the fraud liable for the losses. Thus, companies were put on alert that if they did not exercise "reasonable care," they would be liable for the check fraud losses their banks had been previously eating.

No executive wants to be responsible for such a loss. It's not a resume-building event for an executive planning a climb up the corporate ladder. As a professional working in accounts payable, it's your job to make sure that your controller or chief financial officer (CFO) never has to deal with this career-topping issue.

THE RIGHT WAY

Let's start with the check stock itself. If you are not using laser stock, which has no preprinted information, you need to be concerned about the checks themselves. It should have a number of safety features incorporated in it to make alteration and copying difficult, if not impossible. Changes in the UCC could make organizations liable for fraud against checks if they don't exercise "ordinary care." ANSI standard X9.51 advises that organizations use of at least three security features. The accompanying table lists some that are currently on the market. New features are added regularly.

Ideally, laser checks should be used, as many control problems are eliminated. However, this is not to say that you are not using best practices if you do use preprinted check stock; you just have a larger number of control issues.

Once checks are printed, they need to be signed in many organizations. Some groups have a facsimile signature put on during the check printing process and a second manual signature added for checks over a given dollar amount. The requirement for a second signature varies from company to company, with some requiring a second manual signature on everything (why use the facsimile, then?) to those requiring the second signature only for very large checks.

This second signature requirement introduces problems. First, the checks must be collated with the backup before they are given to the signer. This collating task can take hours or even, in rare cases, days. How the checks are cared for during this process indicates whether the organization has strong internal controls surrounding the process and whether there is the potential for trouble or not. The checks should be held under lock and key with limited access, just like blank preprinted check stock.

Once the checks are signed and ready to be mailed, they should be held in accounts payable until the last possible moment. They should not be taken to the mailroom until the end of the day right before the mail is being taken to the post office. Otherwise, there is the potential for the wrong person to get their hands on your checks. Temporary employees, as well as delivery personnel from all sorts of companies providing services to your company, pass through your mailroom. While most are excruciatingly honest, a few are not—and you have no way of knowing who's who.

There's another touchy issue when it comes to checks that few people focus on. By now, most accounts payable professionals know they should use positive pay and a large percent of organizations actually do use it. Most run the file and send it to the bank as soon as they have printed their checks.

But here's where there could be a problem if you don't use payee name positive pay (and at this point few companies do) and it takes you several days to get checks collated, signed, uncollated, and into the mail. An unscrupulous employee who knew the check numbers and dollar amounts could circumvent your positive pay controls.

While in all likelihood this would happen only once in any organization and the odds are small, it is a risk. Therefore, get your checks into the mail as quickly as possible after the checks are printed. If it is possible to delay the transmission of the positive pay file until the checks are printed, that is probably not a bad idea, although it will require some additional coordination.

THE BEST WAY

Get rid of the paper completely. We're serious. Convert all your suppliers to electronic payments. This effectively eliminates all the problems discussed here. Unfortunately, even the most progressive companies are not able to get away from paper completely. Convert as many payments to electronics as you possibly can and then institute the controls discussed above to minimize the "opportunity for fraud."

QUESTIONS THAT REVEAL YOUR INTERNAL CHECK CONTROLS

If you are not sure whether your controls are adequate, ask yourself the following questions. Your answers will reveal if and where you have concerns.

- Do you have at least three fraud prevention features embedded in your check stock?

- How is your preprinted check stock secured?
- What happens to checks during the collating process?
- How are your checks stored after they are printed but before they are mailed?
- Where are checks kept when sent out for signature?
- How are checks mailed?
- Are checks delivered to the mailroom at the end of the day?
- When do you send the positive pay file to the bank?

BEST CHECK-HANDLING PRACTICES BETWEEN PRINTING AND MAILING

Once the checks are printed, they should be kept with great care until they are mailed. This means that if they are not mailed the same day, they are printed (as they ideally should be) they need to be kept in a secure location. They should not be kept on the credenza of an executive who has to provide a second signature or left lying around the accounts payable department. More than one sticky-fingered employee or cleaning person has walked off with a check that didn't belong to them.

Yes, that means *any* time checks are waiting for a signature or to be mailed, they should be locked back in that secure location where the check stock is stored. Companies that use laser check stock and do not have a secure location, as described earlier, need to create a locked space where checks can be stored after printing and before they are mailed.

MAILING CHECKS

When an invoice is approved for payment, it should have a mailing address on it. Additionally, this address should match the "pay to" address in the master vendor file. Any variation from this should be investigated because it may be the first sign that something is amiss. Under all but the most extenuating circumstances, checks should be mailed. Returning checks to requisitioners causes many problems, one of which is that it makes it easier for an employee to commit fraud.

When checks are mailed, care should be taken regarding when and how this is done. Checks should be sealed in envelopes and delivered either straight to the post office or to the mailroom at the end of the day. If checks are delivered to the mailroom, they should not be left out in the open where anyone walking by can see them and easily take one. This is especially true if temporary employees are frequently used by the company.

Similarly, thought should be given as to whether a window envelope should be used. While window envelopes simplify the mailing of checks, they are also a red flag for a crook looking for checks to steal. Rarely are checks mailed in anything other than window envelopes.

Additionally, if one-part sealers (the multipart forms containing the check) are used, extra care should be taken.

FROM PRINTING TO MAILING: DO YOU KNOW WHERE YOUR CHECKS ARE?

Do you remember the old commercial that asked, "It's 10 PM; do you know where your children are?" Reflect on your paper checks. Do you know where your paper checks are between the time they are printed and when they go to the post office for mailing? If you are not careful, all your strong internal controls will be for naught if someone walks off with a few of your checks.

After Printing and before Signing

Do you collate checks with backup before taking them to be signed? Most organizations do. Depending on the number of checks and your signing requirements, this can be a huge job. I know one organization that can spend two days a week on this odious task. Here are some issues to consider about this part of the process:

- Where are the checks put after printing but before the collating is done?
- Where is the collating done? Out in the open where both employees and visitors frequently walk by, or in a secure location?
- If the collating is not finished by the end of the day, where are the checks kept?
- Who does the collating?
- Where are the checks kept between collating and bringing them to an authorized signer?

When the Checks Are Out for Signing

How often do you walk down the hall and glance into an authorized signer's empty office only to see checks lying on his or her desk? Unfortunately, this is a familiar sight at virtually every organization that has checks manually signed—and it is a risk. Whether a disgruntled employee or one with personal financial issues or an outsider with larceny in his or her heart walks by, these checks are an invitation to potential trouble.

Similarly, when the signer completes his or her task of signing, do they immediately return the checks or call for someone to pick them up? And, if they call for someone, do they stay with the signed checks or just leave them waiting? Should checks be stolen along this part of the operation they would probably clear your bank as the positive pay file is in all likelihood already transmitted. Should the bank ever discover your lax practices, you could be deemed not exercising reasonable care and therefore liable for the loss.

When the Checks Are Signed and Returned

Once the checks are returned, in most organizations, the backup must be removed and the checks put into an envelope for mailing. Is this done immediately, or do the folders with the signed checks lie around for a few hours or days? If the stuffing of the envelopes isn't completed by the close of business, where are those signed checks stored?

This is one of the most critical control points. In most organizations, the positive pay file has been transmitted and the checks are signed and viable. A crook does not have to do much to get the check cashed. It is recommended that these checks be stored under lock and key if they are not mailed immediately.

To be perfectly honest, it is a good idea to keep all checks locked if they are not being worked on. But it is critical if the check has been signed.

And finally, once the checks have been stuffed into their envelopes, are they taken to the mailroom? It is highly recommended that they not be taken to the mailroom until right before the mail goes to the post office. The reason is simple. In many organizations the mailroom has numerous outsiders in and out, making deliveries, picking up packages, and so on. You have no idea who those people are. And, if they happen to have a penchant for check fraud, they will recognize what's in those envelopes you have so nicely lined up for mailing.

As those reading this are ever so painfully aware, you cannot completely stop check fraud. But you can make it more difficult for those looking to perpetrate check fraud on your organization. By appropriately addressing the issue of where your checks are at every step of the cycle, you will have made it all the harder for them. And, hopefully, they will turn their eyes to some other firm.

WIRE TRANSFERS

Occasionally, when check fraud occurs, the company is left scratching its proverbial head trying to figure out how the forger got its bank account number. The answer is simple. Call any treasury or accounts payable department, tell them you are getting ready to wire money to the company, and ask for the company's wire instructions. Nine times out of ten, the person on the other end of the phone would rattle off the organization's wire instructions, not giving the matter a second thought. Included in those wire instructions are the name of the bank the company uses and its bank account number.

That is why many organizations set up a separate account to accept wire transfers and block any checks on that account. At the end of each day, the funds in the wire account are swept into another account for corporate purposes. Thus, even if the crook gets the bank account number for wires, it will not help.

For the same reason, it is recommended that the signatures in the annual report not be the actual signatures of your executives. The forgers could simply get a copy of the annual report and, with the wire instructions, have all the information needed to create a phony check.

REBATE AND REFUND CHECKS

For similar reasons, it is recommended that organizations set up a separate account for rebates and refunds and not honor checks in those accounts over a certain low dollar limit. Set the limit appropriate for your business, possibly as low as $10.

Crooks would order something from a company, overpay for it, and then wait for the refund check to get that all-important bank account number.

RUSH CHECKS

Rush checks, also referred to as emergency checks, priority checks, or ASAP checks, are the bane of many accounts payable departments. They are traditionally manually written, although in recent

years they have been printed by computers and are produced outside the normal check production cycle. They are supposed to be
for those once-in-a-lifetime emergencies that crop up with varying frequency, depending on the nature of the business and the
tolerance of the corporation for this type of behavior. In reality,
they are sometimes written to cover for the sloppy habits of certain employees, such as executives who get behind in their work
and neglect to approve invoices for payment, harried purchasing
managers who lose an invoice in the stacks of paper on their desk,
or late-to-the-game employees who rush in an expense report the
day their credit card bill is due.

And what's even worse is that a large percentage of fraudulent
checks (as well as duplicate payments) are rush checks. How is
this possible? Consider what happens in your organization when
a vendor calls up screaming for payment and threatening to put
the organization on credit hold. In many organizations, especially
those that don't always get their bills paid on time, this is enough to
"stop the presses" and get a rush manual check drawn up, signed,
and mailed. And guess what? Crooks know this, too, and take
advantage of this fact. So, if the inefficiencies in your accounts
payable operation haven't convinced you to prohibit rush checks,
the increased risk for fraud should.

WHY RETURNING CHECKS TO REQUISITIONERS CAN BE A PROBLEM

Checks should not be returned to requesters for two simple reasons:
it's inefficient and it opens the door to fraud. I could write a million
words explaining the inconveniences to accounts payable caused by #7
requests to return checks that might make some impact on a few.
I could write about the potential for fraud in theory and not make
half the impact of the following real-life tale in the words of the
professional who shared the story:

> A former employee, who was in charge of all the trade show plan-
> ning, would request checks to be processed, payable to the trade

shows. The request was approved by the same person, using the initials of their superior. This was common practice at that time, due to the lengthy traveling the superior does. Now when I think about it, how stupid were we to put that much trust in someone? We have a list of people allowed to sign the checks here—none are stamped. Those individuals signed these checks, trusting the former employee, and allowed me to return the checks to her, believing they were getting sent to the trade shows. Never in my wildest dreams did I ever imagine it was possible for a check made payable to another business to be allowed to be deposited into a personal bank account. Five years into the situation, one of the VPs decided to find out why the trade shows were costing so much. We found out why. This ordeal cost the company a lot of money. Since then, we have drastically changed our policies. I will not give any check back to the requester. The only exception to this rule is that specific requests must be signed off by an officer of the company.

This story emphasizes, once again, the old chestnut about fraud being committed by long-term, trusted employees.

HOW COMPANIES HANDLE CHECK RETURN REQUESTS BY REQUISITIONERS

What follows are ways some companies have found to eliminate or minimize the odious practice of returning checks to requisitioners:

- We discourage giving a check to anyone; we state that we prefer to mail it. If we give a check to someone, for security and traceability reasons, we make the individual picking up the check fill out a form stating the reason, print and sign their name, and date.
- We make the requester pick up the check in our department. They must sign for picking up the check. They also have only 24 hours or we put the check in the mail.
- Returning checks to the requisitioner is strictly prohibited at my company unless written permission is granted from the chief financial officer (CFO). People don't even ask because

the answer would be no. If someone needs to send a check with an application or other documentation, we have a system whereby that information is sent to accounts payable and they mail the documentation with the check.

- We almost never release a check to anyone but the person it's made out to. In my six years with this organization, I have never had to process a request to release a payment to anyone else, in fact. The process requires about four levels of approval to do, all the way up to our equivalent of a CFO. The system is so involved that you really have to have an emergency situation to circumvent mailing the payment, and it is usually easier to find another solution than to jump through all those hoops.

- Our policy is that no check payable to a vendor for goods and/or services received is returned to the requester no matter what. For other checks—such as books, dues, and subscriptions—we are working with the requesting department and our internal audit department to have the paperwork that needs to go with the check sent to us and allow us to mail directly from accounts payable. Checks of a sensitive nature (such as legal, insurance, employee related) that have personal information on them are usually returned to the requester so that they can be handled appropriately. We currently process about 2,500 checks per week, and I would say that only 2 percent, maximum, are returned to a department.

- Our policy is to return a check to a requester only if there is documented approval from the requester's director or above. A director in our organization is similar to a controller. It is a pretty high position that usually reports directly to a vice president of the company.

- Our solution is to have a standardized e-mail that tells them the check is ready at a certain location. Then they come and pick it up. Or if they are "above" picking it up, we still send the e-mail but leave it in their centralized mailbox.

- We ask that any backup that needs to be sent with the check be sent to accounts payable along with the invoice. Check copies are kept in a PDF-format file so that anyone wishing to have the check returned to them for the purpose of keeping a copy with their records can request that accounts payable e-mail one off to them.

- Here is a brief overview of our situation: We have initiated a policy stating that all checks will remain with accounting and be mailed with attachments, as provided. All documentation that needs to be sent with the check must be turned in to accounting, and the person assigned to reconcile the check registry attaches the documentation and mails it with the check. This sounds good in theory, but there are always exceptions: checks to be hand delivered, checks to be picked up, and donations, to name a few. We have better control than earlier in the year, but we are still working on the details!

FRAUD IN THE REAL WORLD

Here are some stories from readers and the newspapers illustrating the points made above. To my mind, some of them prove that life is indeed stranger than fiction.

- A department store about 100 miles away from our agency cashed a check that had our name and bank account information on it. Luckily, our bank caught it, so we lost nothing. This incident pushed our organization to start using the positive pay process.

- A manager would submit an invoice for payment and also request that the check be returned to him. He would then cash the check and keep the money. What management did was to declare that checks will be returned only to the vendor and never to the requester. If a check had to be returned to the requester, there had to be an exception form filled out by the CFO.

- Check fraud happened with a carbon checkbook: the check would be written on the ledger, and the carbon image would show $300, with space before the decimal point. Once the check was removed from the checkbook, the actual check was altered, adding another zero or two prior to the decimal, increasing the amount of the check to $3,000 or $30,000. This person also balanced the checkbook and was able to mask this at a company that already had cash flow issues. This trusted employee was already letting ownership know regularly that there was a cash flow issue and would seek and get funding from other sources, so this made it easy to include another $2,700 or so a month. This fraud continued for about 18 months, with the grand total reaching approximately $60,000.

- Someone got hold of one of our checks and recreated it, using a phony vendor and phony check number, but forging the real signatures and account numbers. It was caught because some nice lady received a very large check from us for no good reason that she knew. She called to ask us why we had sent it. Very nice of her; honesty wins out. As it turned out, there were several phony checks that same month, all in all adding to about $125,000. Most had already been cleared. Had we had positive pay, it would not have occurred. We are in the process of implementing positive pay, but this was not the reason—it was already in process. We were fortunate; the bank reimbursed us. The bad guys were caught, and they are in the hands of the authorities. Apparently, they would send checks to random folks via Federal Express and then would steal the envelopes before the people got home. This lady was there to receive the check herself, so we had all the evidence we needed.

- Our office manager had taken checks written for trade show expenses and deposited them into her personal account. None of them were written out to her, but the bank let her deposit them anyway. Since this occurrence, we have tightened our internal controls in all aspects.

- An outside individual used our bank routing and account number on their checks and mailed them out to individuals to cash and then remit a portion to the person who sent them the check via wire. We are not sure how it could have been prevented except for positive pay.

- An employee who stole a check from the bottom of the stack fraudulently signed and cashed it. Since he did the bank reconciliation, he was able to hide the fraud for some time. He was fired, but didn't have to pay the funds back.

- We had an employee who was rushing payments for some of his suppliers. Once he received the signed check, he would then remove the name and add his own to the check. He started out small, but when he was caught they determined it was approximately $120,000 over the year and half this was going on. He was caught only because someone made a keying error and requested a copy of the canceled check. The director happened to turn over the canceled check, and there was the employee's signature. Had he been a little smarter, using another name, he might never have been caught. He was prosecuted and ordered to pay restitution. We collected restitution for a couple of years. Then the crook went to court in Florida and the judge overturned the restitution.

CONCLUDING THOUGHTS

Check fraud, or rather the risk of it, is an issue no organization can afford to ignore. There are just too many ways an unscrupulous individual can take advantage—and the risk is both internal and external. We haven't talked as much in this chapter about segregation of duties and appropriate internal controls, but they are issues to be taken seriously when it comes to your checks because, after all, it is your organization's money, and without it, the organization would cease to exist.

3

CHECK STOCK: STOP THE FRAUDSTERS' PRESSES

As you can see from Chapter 2, crooks can play lots of games with your paper checks. While your best defense might be completely eliminating them, that is not a real option for most organizations at this time. Thus, it is imperative that every organization make their check stock difficult to replicate. There are numerous features that can be included in your checks, and in this chapter we'll talk about some of them as well as what doesn't work.

SECURITY FEATURES IN YOUR CHECK STOCK

Most readers know better than to purchase their checks without security features incorporated into the stock. The list of possible features shown in this chapter can be overwhelming. Clearly, no one in their right mind would include all. We wondered just how many would be considered adequate and effective, so we recruited two industry experts and got their opinions. Trish Hart, Bottom-line Technology's sales manager for the Supplies and Consumables group, and Judy Esguerra, ACOM Solutions, Inc.'s accounting manager, shared their considerable expertise regarding check stock.

How Many Are Enough?

The American National Standards Institute (ANSI) Committee that oversees check-writing standards (ASC X9.B) suggests a minimum of three features for due diligence, says Esguerra. Bottomline also strongly supports ANSI standard X9.51, which advises the use of at least three security features, notes Hart.

When selecting which features to use, Esguerra suggests using a rule of thumb that at least one feature should be overt (visible to the naked eye), one should be covert (not visible to the naked eye), one should be an anticopy feature (a feature designed to hinder duplication), and one should be antialteration (something that deters data modification).

Which Are Most Effective?

The three security features that Bottomline promotes to its customers as a best practice include thermochromic ink, fourdrinier watermarks, and fluorescent and opaque inks, says Hart.

No one feature offers the best protection and all can be defeated, notes Esguerra. This disheartening news is the reason she suggests the best defense is to use a variety of security features in check stock. She points out that multiple features create a web of security that deter many people from even attempting to alter or duplicate a check, and make it very difficult for those who still try.

Esguerra notes that that positive pay is still the best security feature available, because no matter how many physical features you put into a check, they are useless if the bank teller isn't checking for them.

New Security Features

We asked our experts about new security features on the forefront. Hart noted that thermochromic (heat reactive) ink provides good protection against new copier technologies, along with the use of fourdrinier watermark papers, and/or fluorescent and opaque inks. She says these are all image-friendly security options.

Esguerra pointed out that there are several different companies working on an indelible ink solution, as well as others that are attempting to encode pertinent check information into a bar code.

WHAT ELSE?

What this discussion illuminates is the sad reality that crooks continue to look for ways to thwart new advances in check fraud prevention. Hence, it is imperative that our readers continue to be vigilant. Hart points out that even the best security measures, including positive pay, will not stop check fraud completely.

"Use positive pay; keep your check stock in a secure, locked location; and perform regular audits and reconciliations of your accounts," says Esguerra.

The best defense, notes Hart, is to move away from paper checks and migrate as much as possible to more secure, less costly electronic payment methods such as automated clearinghouse (ACH), wires, and purchasing cards.

Both experts offer excellent closing advice. They advocate the use of these security measures, which, when used properly, will limit a company's liability if check fraud does occur. Make sure that you have ample security features so that the responsibility for fraud is on the bank of first deposit, not you, they advise. We couldn't have said it better ourselves.

SOME CHECK FRAUD SECURITY FEATURES

Following is a list of some of the security features that are currently available for purchase, to be embedded in your check stock:

- *American Banking Association (ABA) check endorsement clause.* The ABA endorsement clause is printed on the back of the check and verifies the colored check stock and pantographic background.

- *Antisplice backer.* Horizontal or diagonal lines of varying thicknesses that are printed on the back, making it difficult to alter information by the cut-and-paste method.
- *Artificial watermarks.* These watermarks are subtly printed logos or words that can be viewed at a 45-degree angle. This check fraud prevention technique is designed to defeat the person using a copier or scanner on your business check. Copiers and scanners are designed to capture images at 90-degree angles. A 45-degree angle watermark may not be reproduced by copying or scanning. Your bank can review your laser check and notice the inclusion or absence of the watermark.
- *Chemical-reactive paper.* This paper shows stains or spots when an attempt is made to remove the check information with chemical ink eradicators or manual erasure. When "washing" a check to commit check fraud, the most common acetate used is fingernail polish remover. Using chemical-reactive paper for your business check and blank laser check may defeat those people looking to alter your checks by chemical means.
- *Endorsement pantograph/copy void.* Single-color pantograph makes the endorsing signature difficult, if not impossible, to scan or copy. This area also has a copier-void feature built into the background. Note: Not always effective.
- *Erasure protection.* When areas on the front of your business check are erased, the colored pantograph becomes white. The pantograph may defeat the person looking to commit check fraud on your laser check by a manual erasure process.
- *Invisible and fluorescent fibers.* These fibers are embedded in your business check and can be seen only under an ultraviolet light (black light). A fraudulent check will not contain these

invisible fibers. All banks now scan checks under ultraviolet light before processing for payment.

- *Laid lines.* Varying-size lines are printed across the back of the check, so any part of the check that is removed and replaced will be obvious. # 9

- *Magnetic ink character recognition (MICR) band.* This band creates a clear zone for the MICR line on your check. The banking community has requested a clear space to be added for the MICR check line. This MICR band appears as a one-half-inch space between the bottom of the pantograph and the bottom of the check. The MICR band allows for a lower reject rate when your bank scans your MICR check.

- *MICR target alignment.* This is a box added to position 43 of the MICR area for guidance in printing the bank routing transit number on your business check.

- *Microprinting.* Microprint is very small type in the check border and the back of the check signature line. This microprint can be read only with a magnifying glass. When a person attempts to commit check fraud by copying or scanning the check, the microprint text becomes a solid line. Your bank can look at your business check and see that the microprint text no longer exists.

- *Non-negotiable stub backer.* "Non-negotiable" is printed on the back of the check stub to prevent fraudulent use of the check stock.

- *Padlock security icon.* Located in two places: on the front of the check, alerting the teller that there are security features to look for; and on the bottom of the back of the check, stating that there are additional security features embedded within the check design.

- *Pantograph.* A pantograph in your check stock background complicates alteration and unauthorized reproduction. The pantograph is designed to make blank laser checks and business checks difficult for the forger to alter and copy.

- *Rainbow prismatic colored stock.* Gradient colors are difficult to photocopy accurately.
- *Sequential numbering.* Located on the back of the check stock.
- *Security feature box.* Describes some of the visible and hidden security features.
- *Security screen.* An example of a security screen is the words *Original Document* on the back of your check stock offset against a gray background. This offset print makes it difficult to copy or scan your laser business check.
- *Simulated watermark.* Printed with white ink, simulated watermarks have a different reflectance than the base paper and can be seen at an angle. Because the ink is white, it cannot be photocopied or scanned.
- *Void pantograph (also referred to as copier-void design).* If your laser-generated business check is photocopied or scanned, the word *Void* appears on the copied check. The face of this blank check document contains a colored background without the word *Void*. Unfortunately, some of the newer model copiers can now defeat the void pantograph. A knowledgeable individual can adjust a new-generation copier to the specific attributes of your business check.
- *Warning box (sometimes referred to as endorsement warning).* A warning box on back of the check lists the check's security features and describes how to detect fraud and alterations.
- *Watermark certification seal.* A seal that certifies all legal ANSI and ABA specifications for check printing have been met. These watermarks on the back of the check cannot be photocopied.

A WORD ABOUT VOID PANTOGRAPHS

Here's the simple fact. With the right copier, void pantographs don't work. And we are not talking about expensive technology. In many cases, we're referring to the $500 copier you just purchased at Staples. This phenomenon is not something cooked up by crooks trying to get around your fraud deterrents; it is simply an unfortunate victim as technology gets better and cheaper. We spoke with several experts as well as practitioners about the situation, and we're afraid we're going to have to ring the death knell on what was once a great check fraud deterrent.

Void pantographs have become especially vulnerable with the technological improvements to copiers. There have been a number of documented cases in which the void pantographs disappear. The disappearance usually depends on the specific copier settings. Unfortunately, you have no control over what settings a crook can and cannot use on a copier. This is an unfortunate side effect—the positive improvements in copier technology have had a negative effect on check imaging.

At least one check-printing company wants its customers to understand that the technology may no longer work. Hence, it requires that customers sign off on the void, confirming that they have read its disclaimer that the void is a defeatable technology.

VOID PANTOGRAPHS AND POSITIVE PAY

We've heard from several people that their banks complained about the void pantograph interfering with their positive pay. This is a bigger issue than just the void pantograph, but it is something to consider when deciding what security features to include in your checks.

What banks really want are checks with backgrounds that totally "drop out." This gives the bank a clear and concise image to enable positive pay without interference. This additional pressure from the banks is another reason void pantographs will eventually disappear as a standard check security feature.

Readers should keep this comment in mind when they are ordering new check stock. While a hued background composed of your company's name or logo might be desirable from a corporate image standpoint, it could cause similar problems with your bank.

FRAUD IN THE REAL WORLD

We have had our checks washed and the vendor names and amounts changed. We caught these using positive pay, which verifies both the name and amount. The fraud in our case was detected by our positive pay bank. We wrote a check for $3,000 and the recipient tried to cash it for $30,000.

CONCLUDING THOUGHTS

As you can see, there's a lot that can be done to play with your paper checks. It is up to every organization to make it difficult for the crooks who manage to get their hands on one of your checks. By selectively including security features to include in your checks, you have done just that.

4

P-CARD: NOT AS BIG AN ISSUE AS YOU MIGHT THINK

Purchase card (p-card) fraud by employees doesn't happen often, but it does happen occasionally. In fact, despite the copious statistics found in various studies and quoted throughout this book, none of the studies broke out p-card fraud. This is because, at least at this point in time, p-card fraud has not gotten out of hand. Often, we hear stories of executives reluctant to undertake a p-card program because of the fear their employees will go wild with the cards, spending on personal items and running up huge bills for which the organization will be responsible. While this has happened in a few rare instances, those occasions are rare. What's more, every organization with a program can put in place relatively easily controls and limits that will prevent this from happening.

PRINTING OF THE INVOICE

This is an ongoing problem, and it does not appear to be going away. There are a few vendors who, for technical reasons, cannot suppress the printing and mailing of an invoice. It is likely you will receive invoices from a few vendors who have already been paid with a p-card. A close inspection of the invoice will show that it has been marked paid, but all too often, those statements are in small print and are missed by the person processing the invoice.

Thus, even though your 100 percent above-board employee does nothing wrong, an invoice may be sent for an item that was paid for at the point of purchase. Is this fraud? Usually not. However, there are vendors who take advantage, knowing processors don't look at the fine print, especially when the dollar amount is small.

And then there are the unscrupulous vendors who send the invoice even though they know they've been paid. Sometimes this is done in collusion with an employee, but more often it is not. Controls in this arena nip two problems in the bud: duplicate payments and fraud.

START OFF ON THE RIGHT FOOT

One of the best ways to prevent fraud is to make employees aware of the consequences before using the card the first time. The most successful way to do this is to have them sign a letter indicating that they understand they will be immediately terminated if the card is used inappropriately. Then, if an employee does misuse the card, follow through—and don't keep it a secret. This may sound harsh, but if employees realize the organization means business, they are less likely to try something inappropriate.

If the supervisor is ultimately accountable for how the card is used, and he or she should be, have the supervisor sign the agreement as well. This reminds them of their responsibilities and obligations related to each card. Each level of monitoring in a card program is one more way to minimize potential misuse or abuse.

Policies and procedures with strong internal controls should be established and shared with all affected parties. Otherwise, each will do as they please and that can only lead to trouble.

POLICY AND PROCEDURES MANUAL

Writing detailed policies and procedures, publishing them in a manual and on your web site for everyone to see, and updating them regularly makes it difficult for an employee to claim they "didn't know" that something was against policy. It is also at the heart of your fraud prevention program.

The written policy should:

- List prohibited uses.
- Include instructions for what to do when the card is lost.
- Spell out cardholder responsibilities.
- Indicate any and all approvals required.
- Discuss monitoring.
- Provide information about required training.

The policy should also include steps to be taken when an employee leaves the company or is terminated. Procedures should be worked out with human resources to allow for the immediate notification of the termination of any employee who is a cardholder. This will allow for the immediate cancellation of the terminated employee's card.

SPELL OUT CONSEQUENCES

A meaningful policy concerning consequences for misuse of the card should be spelled out and enforced across the board. This means your executives as well as the rank and file. Once it becomes known—and it will—that a senior-level executive was not reprimanded over misuse of the card, all cardholders will feel that they don't have to stick to the guidelines.

Uniform enforcement is crucial. Any misuse of a p-card should be treated as a violation, and proven use of a p-card for personal purchases should be treated like any other type of fraud, with the fraudster prosecuted and the prosecution publicized. Not prosecuting and publicizing thefts and their consequences reinforces bad behavior with the card and will result in more fraud. The likelihood of detection and punishment for theft acts as a very real fraud deterrent.

REQUIRE DOCUMENTATION

#12

Your documentation in the p-card world is the receipt. These should be maintained by the employee or sent in to accounts payable, depending on your policy. At a minimum, they should be spot checked. If you have any employees known to be loose in their approach to your spending policies, their receipts should be checked 100 percent of the time. Not surprisingly, these will probably be the same employees whose expense reports are checked thoroughly.

When receipts are checked, make sure none have been altered and that they are for appropriate purchases. While an occasional missing receipt is to be expected, be suspicious of any employee who regularly "loses" receipts.

Ultimately, all expenditures should be approved by the purchasing employee's superior. Make it part of your policy that the manager is responsible for these purchases as well as the employee. Too often, managers sign whatever is pushed in front of them, especially if the purchases are made by long-term, trusted employees. As *Accounts Payable Now & Tomorrow*'s readers are only too aware, these are the individuals most likely to commit fraud.

Thus, an auditing program to monitor for indiscretions is a good idea. Surprise audits by the internal audit team is another way to prevent duplicity. While it is not possible to audit all expenditures, a small portion can be checked. When the audit is complete, send notes to all whose purchases were checked, saying, "Congratulations, your recent p-card purchase activity was reviewed by internal audit and you passed." Let word of mouth about these notes do the talking for you.

DON'T OVERLOOK RECEIPTS

Whether receipts are kept in the possession of the purchaser or turned over to the administrator, original receipts for every p-card purchase made should be kept. If they stay with the purchaser, a certain number should be verified randomly each month.

Obviously, a photocopy of a receipt is not acceptable as documentation. In the electronic age, it is more difficult to obtain original vendor documentation, and duplicates looking like originals are easy to obtain. Still, make it part of your policy that original receipts are required wherever possible.

ROLE OF A PROGRAM ADMINISTRATOR IN FRAUD PREVENTION

A permanent administrator with responsibility for, and authority over, the p-card program should be appointed. Without a dedicated administrator who assures that cardholders are trained and card usage is monitored, your program is likely to flounder. He or she will make sure all aspects of the card program are kept up to date and reflect the most current technology. He or she will also be responsible for seeing that management controls and fraud monitoring are in place.

The administrator should be responsible for card distribution, training, and retraining. This training should be for both cardholders and transaction reconcilers.

APPROVALS AND COMPLIANCE

Proper approvals need to be obtained every step of the way. This means any time a new card is issued, it needs an approval. Similarly, do not overlook card issues when employees leave your employ. Make sure the card is retrieved and canceled, especially if the employee has left under less-than-optimum circumstances. This last step is often lost in the shuffle. More than a few accounts payable professionals report that they often learn weeks after the fact about the departure of an employee.

No employee should be able to use the card willy-nilly without someone looking over their purchases and reviewing their receipts and/or statements. The reviewer should also be responsible for ensuring policy compliance.

ROLE OF LIMITS WITH RESPECT TO FRAUD

It is possible to set individual limits on each card. These are a great way to greatly minimize the risk of fraud. If someone has a $500 monthly limit on his or her card, there's not much damage they can do. Similarly, if appropriate, a $100 daily limit will go a long way to minimizing any potential damage. Establish reasonable card limits to reduce excessive or inappropriate use.

A reasonable rule of thumb is to provide card limits that slightly exceed the highest actual purchase in the preceding year by a card-holder. Limits should be defined by employee or by employee class or use. Don't establish blanket limits for all cards. This will give some individuals considerably more purchasing power than they will ever need or use, thus increasing the risk of fraud with no added benefit to the organization.

Some organizations further limit the use of the card by blocking Merchant Category Codes (MCC) codes on some or all cards. While this is great when it comes to fraud, it sometimes presents logistical issues. Each company is assigned one MCC code, even though it may be in multiple lines of business. Generally, the company picks its main line for establishing the MCC code. If that is a code you have blocked on your cards, your cardholders could run into difficulty when they go to make a purchase.

TRAIN, TRAIN, AND THEN TRAIN AGAIN

Perhaps the best way to guard against inappropriate use of the card is to provide cardholder training for new employees as well as anyone who hasn't used the card in a while. In fact, many organizations with successful programs require retraining on an annual basis. The experts recommend that this training be face to face, at least for the initial training.

WHAT ABOUT INAPPROPRIATE USE?

The fraud issue becomes murky when it comes to expense control. Rogue spenders sometimes make it difficult to discern inappropriate use from that which is fraudulent. Some of what might be considered inappropriate may simply be the result of lax management and review. Still, if a company is trying to rein in costs and make use of preferred suppliers to earn quantity discounts, rogue spending with nonpreferred vendors can be problematic.

Similarly, if the rogue purchaser goes to another vendor, the issue of overpaying or fraud can come into play—although it is tricky to discern. Variances from the approved routine make it easier for a thieving employee to commit fraud.

Transaction splitting should also cause some concern. This is one way employees get around preset spending limits. The limits were put in place for a purpose, not so some clever employee could devise a way to circumvent them. Rarely is there a good reason for this.

P-cards are a terrific tool. They help smooth the payment process, allowing staff to focus on larger-dollar invoices. With the proper controls, they can be wonderful. In the hands of a crook, however, they can lead to disaster. Following the procedures discussed above will help ensure that it doesn't happen on your watch.

Cardholders should not under any circumstances:

- Share their card with other employees.
- Use the card for personal purchases (although some companies do allow this).
- Split transactions (often as a way to get around limits).

FRAUD IN THE REAL WORLD

Here are some stories from readers and the newspapers illustrating the points made in this chapter. To my mind, some of them prove that life is indeed stranger than fiction.

- An employee used his p-card to guarantee a high-dollar car for his personal use. His position was not one that required a company vehicle, plus when the charges posted, one charge exceeded the single purchase and monthly purchase limit. The employee was terminated, his p-card was canceled, and the police were involved on behalf of the car rental agency. The company withheld as much of the final pay as the government allows, and we were able to recoup the balance from the credit card company because of the documentation we provided and the steps we took according to our contract with them.

- A fleet fuel card was used by a former employee. Since there was no way to prove exactly who used the card, we were not able to prosecute and simply closed the card to avoid future "losses."

- In one well-publicized U.S. federal agency case, a person from Los Alamos National Laboratory who had a high five-figure p-card limit was accused of trying to negotiate the purchase of a Ford Mustang on his card.

- A college administrator used state purchasing cards to take as much as $350,000 over a six-year period. This administrator used the state-issued cards, which function like credit cards and are billed to government agencies, and submitted fraudulent invoices to conceal personal purchases to take the money between 2001 and 2007.

- A handful of Navy cardholders used government-issued credit cards to buy jewelry, gamble, and even hire prostitutes.

- In other publicized instances, individuals used federal government p-cards for large personal or luxury purchases and even cosmetic surgery.

CLOSING THOUGHTS

P-cards are a wonderful tool for organizations of all sorts looking for ways to streamline purchasing and make the accounts payable function more efficient. The stories of misuse and fraud will make your hair stand on end. But these instances are few and far between. With proper controls, oversight, and monitoring, the cards can be controlled and fraud will be almost nonexistent. So, don't let the few bad apples scare you away from establishing a card program. Simply employ the appropriate controls and enjoy all the benefits.

5

ELECTRONIC PAYMENT FRAUD: NOT A GROWTH INDUSTRY—YET!

If you are not currently making payments via the automated clearinghouse (ACH), do not think you do not have to read this chapter. You are just as vulnerable to ACH fraud as those who do take advantage of electronic payments, and it is crucial that you take the appropriate actions to protect yourself. This is an issue for every organization with a bank account.

Payment fraud via the ACH, while it is not nearly as large a problem as check fraud, is a serious issue. Savvy payment professionals understand that they must take care to ensure that their companies are not victimized by crooks who know their way around computers and the banking system. Aiding in that effort, banks and several service providers are now working to develop products to help thwart this type of crime. What follows is a roundup of the products on the market and coming to market.

ACH BLOCKS

This is the simplest of all the products to use. It allows companies to notify their banks that ACH debits should not be allowed on certain accounts. With this in place, no ACH debit—even one that is authorized—will be able to get through on a given account.

Organizations are advised to put these in place on all accounts where ACH activity is not likely to be used. Readers using this handy tool are advised to keep track of which accounts they have put blocks on. Otherwise, they could end up with egg on their face when a vendor is given authorization to use an ACH debit and everyone has forgotten that the block was put on the account a year or two earlier.

For some time this was the only tool available to block unauthorized ACH transactions and many organizations put them on all accounts. Many companies put ACH blocks on all accounts but one, thus enabling them to accommodate a few vendors (or taxing authorities) that insisted on using an ACH debit.

If your organization was one of those that put blocks on numerous accounts, you should periodically review which accounts have blocks on them and whether or not they still make sense.

ACH FILTERS

An ACH filter allows an organization to give its banks a list of companies authorized to debit its accounts. The banks will then "filter" incoming debits and allow through only those who are on the list submitted earlier. This filter does not check for dollar amounts or whether the particular transaction has been authorized, only that the company doing the debiting is on the approved list.

Readers should be aware that this product is sometimes referred to as ACH positive pay, although in this writer's mind that is not the correct appellation. The line gets blurred even further because some banks match the identities of those attempting to debit an account with those on the list provided by the company and exceptions are reported to the customer to review before payment. Only authorized electronic transactions are allowed to be withdrawn from your account.

ACH POSITIVE PAY

A robust positive pay product for the ACH environment is not universally available today—but it is on its way. We surveyed a number of banks about this issue and found that the products are basically blocks and filters. However, we expect this to change in the very near future, perhaps even by the time you read this book. Check with your bankers on a regular basis to see what new developments they are making in this area.

PAYMENT ACCOUNT DATA: IS IT ACCURATE?

Technology solves a lot of problems, but sometimes it creates new issues or worsens old ones. In this case we're talking about the veracity of bank account information provided by vendors looking for payment. How can you tell if it is accurate, regardless of whether the misinformation is due to human error or fraud? This is not only an accounts payable issue; it is also an internal audit concern.

The Problem

This issue was raised by an internal auditor who wrote, "I'd like some guidance on an issue we are struggling with. The issue is independent verification of payment instructions. When setting up or changing payment instructions in the vendor/supplier master file, we are requiring validation and independent verification of the electronic payee/payment data by someone other than the individual creating the data. This is to avoid fraudulent or incorrect bank accounts entered into the master file, and paid by ACH, and so forth to a fraudster."

He is rightly concerned about someone's simply sending a bank account number change request on a letterhead and having that information entered in the address book system, causing payments to be sent to the new address. A crooked employee could simply supply his or her own bank account information.

A related issue is that even the most honest employee sometimes makes mistakes and could inadvertently transpose two digits when supplying the bank account number, be it the first time or for a legitimate change.

The Solution

This auditor suggests that some sort of verification should take place—and he is not off base. He advocates including a callback to the payee to verify the data, comparison to independent market sources, or verification to authorized signed documentation, and so forth.

This callback procedure is to avoid the risk of simply accepting a bank account add change advised on a letterhead, which could be easily created anywhere by anyone. But this solution is not without its own headaches, which is why few organizations actually bother with it. Independent verification often is not able to be performed, as some payees are difficult to contact, independent sources are not available to verify bank accounts, and so forth. This is why many experts recommend getting a voided check or deposit slip.

There is one other control that we recommend: A very senior officer reviews *all* changes made to the master vendor file. Most controllers don't like this, but it makes your own employees think twice before playing games with the file. Of course, this last step will do little to thwart the fraudulent activities on the part of your vendors' employees.

While at first glance this does not appear to be a master vendor file issue, when you realize it relates to the "remit to" information, it becomes clear that it is.

These solutions demonstrate how important it is not to randomly adopt new processes without thinking through all the ramifications of the new process. The solution, while not ideal, does provide some protection against both fraud and honest mistakes.

ACH DATA ACCURACY: REAL-LIFE SOLUTIONS TO A VERY PRACTICAL PROBLEM

Do you make payments to vendors via the ACH? Have you ever considered whether the account information provided by the vendor is accurate or perhaps some thieving employee has substituted his or her bank account number in place of the vendor's account number? The prenote activity only verifies that the routing and account number are valid—not that the account number matches the vendor name. This issue was brought to our attention by a professional who posed several excellent questions. Specifically, she asked:

- What can prevent an employee from providing their personal bank information as if they were a vendor?
- What about including a fraudulent manually printed check with a fake vendor name?
- How do we ensure the funds we are transferring actually go to the payee intended?

We asked our always thoughtful e-zine readers how they addressed these very pertinent issues. "We are stumped, too," wrote another e-zine reader. "We feel that we are doing all that we can at this point and would be very interested in hearing what others are doing," she added, concerned that her firm might have a material weakness in their processes.

Basic Approach

Several accounts payable managers report using variations of the voided check approach. They have a form for the vendor to fill out and request a voided check along with it. The reason is simple. Quite frequently, people transpose numbers, and a few can't tell the difference between their account number and the bank's transit and routing number.

Restricted Basic Approach

"There's no way to prevent every incident of fraud. The best you can do is make a reasonable effort to obtain/verify accurate information and trust the vendor is looking for the payments and would let you know if they are not being received," notes Monarch Life's assistant vice president and assistant treasurer Robin Roy.

Before paying any vendor by ACH, Monarch requires the vendor to complete a sign-up form and send a voided business check. That's a must, notes Roy. The organization offers ACH payments only to vendors it uses on a regular basis. Their sign-up form requests:

- Payee name
- DBA (if applicable)
- Address
- Business phone number
- Company contact
- Contact's phone number
- Bank name
- Bank address
- Account number
- ABA number
- Authorized company officer's signature

Incorporating a Billing Requirement

An accounting supervisor says her group sends a wire/ACH only to the bank information written on the invoice. She notes that occasionally they will get an e-mail from a vendor requesting that payments be sent to another bank account. She tells them that for control purposes the company has to send it to the bank listed on the invoice.

If the bank information has been changed on the invoice, then it would be caught when the vendor eventually calls to find out why the invoice hasn't been paid. Of course, that is after the fact. If the invoice isn't valid to begin with, then there are control problems—whether the invoice was paid by check or ACH/wire. These are more basic and need to be addressed outside the ACH process.

Put the Onus Back on the Vendor

Another firm takes a different approach. At this organization, the vendor sets up their account information and keeps it updated. They submit invoices, and the accounts payable department creates an electronic batch that gets released by an authorized check signer several times a week.

When the check goes to the vendor's bank, they get a remittance e-mail. The accounts payable associates do not have rights to view the vendor information in the electronic payment system. It is separate from the accounts payable system. Thus, if fraudulent information is entered, it is due to a weakness on the vendor's side, not the customer's.

Incorporating Some Fraud Checking

When the University of Central Florida initiated ACH payments, fraud prevention was high on their list. John Stevens, the University's assistant controller, established quite an elaborate investigation procedure to try to eliminate any fraud. Some of the steps he takes are:

1. Compare the name and address information to the W-9 form on file from previous vendor activity.
2. Compare this information with what is in the vendor database file and resolve any address changes, and so forth.

3. The University requires a voided check or bank letter to be sent along with the application. The information on the check is compared with the information on the application.
4. There are companies that will verify the bank associated with any ABA number, so that can be compared to the banking information on the voided check. If a fraudster were to change the ABA number but leave all other information the same, it would be caught using this method.
5. The University also sends out payment confirmations by e-mail so that, unless the fraudster provides both the wrong banking information *and* his or her own e-mail address, the company will discover a payment has been made but did not get into their account.

He notes that the fraud would be detected in fairly short order when the company submits another invoice for payment and learns that payment has already been made. He is a bit surprised that a lot of companies just ask to have the form completed without any other information.

Finally, he notes that "we are not going to eliminate all fraud. We just need to make it so difficult that the fraudster will find it easier to try another company." We couldn't agree more.

CPA'S PERSPECTIVE

Note that if the funds did go to the wrong party, organizations with even a modicum of controls in place would discover the fraud relatively quickly. Of course, it should be mentioned that the money would be gone by then.

I spoke with Sean Mills, a certified public accountant (CPA) at St. Joseph's Hospital, about these issues. He provides a CPA's outlook on this, not necessarily an existing policy perspective. His useful comments follow.

What can prevent an employee from providing their personal bank information as if they were a vendor? #16

- Request manager name and signature—when you receive information, call back the manager to confirm.
- If the invoices are legitimate, there is a natural control in place; when the vendor is not paid, they are going to be calling; make sure to review statements.
- To ensure the invoice is legitimate, make sure you have a purchase order (PO) process in place and management verification and signature for non-PO items.

How about including a fraudulent manually printed check with a fake vendor name?

- Positive pay is a great first line of defense; a supervisor should also compare manual checks (which should be minimized) submitted to positive pay against original copies.
- To ensure the invoice is legitimate, make sure you have a PO process in place and management verification and signature for non-PO items.
- Management review of expenses and account reconciliations are a great control as well—*conscientious* managers will know if they have been charged for expenses they did not incur. Managers should be provided with accounts payable detail to help them see what is being charged to their accounts.

How do we ensure that the funds we are transferring actually go to the payee intended?

- If the invoices are legitimate, there is a natural control in place; when the vendor is not paid, they are going to be calling; make sure to review statements. I see this as a "check lost in the mail" scenario. Make sure you have a good banking partner; if they make an error, they should fix it. If you have been provided bank information by the vendor, and they confirm the prenote, this really should be all they need—it will be the vendor's responsibility to notify you if they change banking information.

FRAUD IN THE REAL WORLD

An employee wired money to a vendor that happened to be a stock agency. He told the vendor to further fund a certain account, which was his account. He came clean the next morning and was fired.

CLOSING THOUGHTS

While ACH fraud at this point is not a huge issue, we do expect it to grow as fraudsters become more familiar with the approach and check use declines. As you can see, there are many "opportunities" for a fraudster who finds an organization with poor internal controls in this arena. This is one area where organizations are especially vulnerable to game playing by employees who understand the system and can readily identify any weaknesses. Don't let them find those opportunities in your procedures.

Professionals everywhere mustn't ignore this issue, especially if they are not currently making electronic payments, but should incorporate appropriate controls and keep updated on new fraud prevention and detection advances as they become available.

6

DESKTOP FRAUD: FEW THINK ABOUT THIS—BUT EVERYONE SHOULD

Many professionals don't realize the loophole left open for fraud in the use of desktop applications. Few of us could get along in the business world without Excel, and many rely heavily on Access and other desktop applications. While we build in all sorts of controls in other pieces of the business process, when it comes to your desktop applications, many never give the control issue a second thought. Without spilling all our real-life stories, let me point out that there are some in the financial community who believe the 7 billion euro fraud committed at Société Générale in early 2008 was abetted by desktop fraud! Now these are numbers that will get anyone's attention.

EXAMPLE

If you are scratching your head, wondering what the issue really is, consider the following real-life fraud that was uncovered by Pinpoint Profit Recovery Services' Bob Lovallo. Much of the information in this chapter is based on intelligence provided by Lovallo.

Some firms track their escheatable items on an Excel spreadsheet. When bank accounts are closed, as they inevitably are, outstanding checks have to be dealt with. Some organizations leave the accounts open until all the checks clear. Typically, a few checks are never cashed. After proper research, they may be deemed escheatable. In this case, the appropriate information was entered onto an Excel spreadsheet, the accounting entries made, and at the appropriate time the items were turned over to the state. "So, what's the problem?" you ask.

At the firm in question, someone was changing the entries on the Excel spreadsheets. The change did not cost the company a red cent, so its financial records were never affected. What some fraudster was doing was changing the name of the company to whom the funds were owed to the name of an individual. If this "adjustment" had not been detected, the individual would have been able to collect the funds free and clear from the state and no one would have been the wiser.

Could this happen at your company? This is just one example of a transaction that would typically fly under the radar in many organizations. Clearly, a process to ensure the integrity and accuracy of the data in your desktop applications should be a high priority.

OVERVIEW

Any organization wishing to protect itself will typically ensure the correctness of its source data, internal operations, and output by testing mainframe, server, Web applications, and upgrades for evidence of external and internal controls before going live with the applications. Similarly, the controls surrounding these applications, as well as general accounts payable policies and procedures, have come under closer scrutiny in light of Sarbanes-Oxley. But what about your desktop applications—what testing and reviews take place around those functions?

We're talking about those small local processes or workarounds maintained on a desktop such as home-grown custom applications, spreadsheets, and databases that crop up in many organizations where the output is used to determine a company disbursement.

Normally, disbursement data is entered in, and resides on, an online accounts payable application, where formal and applicable disbursement controls are in place. However, when the accounts payable data source from a desktop application does not contain essential business controls and documented procedures, then there is a real exposure to both fraud and inaccurate payments.

ISSUES

Here are some of the issues every manager whose employees use desktop applications needs to consider:

- Are your critical disbursement-sensitive data and files residing on a desktop computer secure enough to prevent the introduction of improper data or revision of proper data?
- Are the data and files protected to prevent unauthorized access, which can lead to and result in a fraud?
- Is there an audit trail and controls in place that support the integrity of source data and file additions, changes, deletions, and output?
- Do you have an inventory list of such sensitive disbursement files and applications?
- If you do have an inventory, have you performed an ongoing security check and audit for data integrity by determining the correctness of the source data?
- Do your desktop procedures include a flow chart indicating what control points are in place to ensure that control and auditability is evident and maintained?
- Do your procedures also address and maintain appropriate segregation of duties?
- Have you tested a portion of original source documents, formulas, report computations, and controls to the desktop application's output?

It is important that information at every step of the process have the appropriate controls in place. You will need to verify the input, the calculations, and the output.

RECOMMENDATION

To get the fraud-prevention ball rolling on your desktop applications, a formal audit review process should take place on a periodic basis. Its purpose is to verify that "desktop applications" have met control assessment criteria by inspection and certify that the application output provides accurate data to accounts payable. This will better protect the company against fraud.

The inspection or review should contain a formal rating for the controls and auditability found in the application, so management can be made aware of any control problems and their severity. The bottom line is that a structured application review and post-review audit report process needs to be adopted. It should assess the adequacies of desktop application control points and audit trails to confirm that the application is doing what it is supposed to do.

If the reviewers identify specific control problems, they should recommend what corrective actions the application owner must take to eliminate the application control weaknesses and ensure that those steps are taken. Often, the authority to implement this type of review lies outside the accounts payable department. Only the controller or chief financial officer (CFO) or an authorized designee with that high level of authority can add and enforce these additional controls to desktop applications. If management is willing to take action, they can better protect themselves and the company against fraud and erroneous payments; in most companies, such small desktop applications receive little or no financial management visibility.

LOVALLO'S GUIDELINES

Without proper controls and oversight, accounts payable—and its financial spreadsheets—is completely unprotected from fraud or serious errors. In the course of my career, I have uncovered spreadsheet fraud and numerous spreadsheet errors that could have been easily prevented if just some basic controls had been incorporated.

We all agree that such desktop tools are too valuable a resource not to be used in today's day-to-day operations. Yet we sometimes rush their implementation, or we've become so accustomed to their presence that we may not have properly protected them from tampering and errors. So where do we start? Pinpoint's Lovallo recommends the following guidelines:

- *Use your street smarts.* We all realize that larcenous individuals who see or can create an opportunity will attempt to commit fraud. We should also understand that computer-centric fraud often shows that the person responsible for the fraud may be the very person who established the system or spreadsheet and/or now controls its operations and modifications. If you have worked in financial management positions, you know that your staff has a high degree of latitude in working with and creating spreadsheets. So it never hurts to periodically spend the time to satisfy yourself that the internal and user controls regarding the desktop computing environment are being properly implemented.

- *Incorporate appropriate segregation of duties.* One major deficiency I've observed is giving one person full responsibility for the control and modification of spreadsheets used within a disbursement process. Segregation of duties is a fundamental and basic concept of internal control that reduces the opportunity for fraud.

- *Verify controls.* Not verifying that internal controls actually exist and are present within the spreadsheet or desktop application is another common flaw. Untested spreadsheets and desktop applications can result in design flaws that result in miscalculations (overpayments), mechanical and/or logic errors (overpayments), lack of or incomplete audit trails, balancing and reconciliation anomalies, or even fraud.

- *Document your processes.* Supporting the desktop spreadsheet application with current and thorough desk procedures is another basic internal control. I have found written procedures surrounding the spreadsheet application that are incomplete or vague. How modifications are to be made and approved for application security should be clearly spelled out.

- *Monitor desktop applications.* As I perform disbursement recovery reviews, I like to help my clients strengthen their internal controls surrounding the use of desktop accounts payable spreadsheet applications. I find that management can be convinced that desktop applications must be monitored, and I often recommend they begin by adopting a more formal and structured top-down approach. Start by establishing accountability.

- *Establish departmental standards for new applications.* Adopt written standards and procedures for developing new applications, addressing their layout, documentation, internal controls, testing, modification, security, and staff activities. Once these are adopted, they will be ready to incorporate into all new desktop applications.

BRINGING IT ALL TOGETHER

Before implementation, however, it's a must to conduct an independent application/spreadsheet assessment to ensure that they possess the necessary internal controls, security, and data integrity and adhere to those established standards and procedures. Next, identify and correct all major deficiencies; then, confirm that all corrections were properly made. This closes the internal control loop from development to implementation.

But it doesn't end there. Monitoring ongoing activities involving desktop applications is the last component of good internal controls in this area. Periodic monitoring determines whether desktop spreadsheets or applications are operating as intended and whether modifications or corrective actions are necessary.

Finally, remember, controls over end-user or desktop computing environments are only as good as those instituted.

FRAUD IN THE REAL WORLD

Here are some stories from readers and the newspapers illustrating the points made above. To my mind, some of them prove that life is indeed stranger than fiction.

- This fraud demonstrates what can happen when lack of segregation of duties and a "trusted employee" are given free rein. The son of a local politician was given a job in the state's unclaimed property office. He took advantage of an apparently lax system where he was responsible for both processing claims and issuing checks—a definite segregation-of-duties conflict. Once he processed a claim, two levels of supervisors were supposed to verify its legitimacy. But his supervisors "trusted him" and performed only a cursory review of the paperwork. The thief also had the computer password for one of his supervisors and used it at times to verify the fake claims he was putting through. The supervisor's password was the word *password*.
- A theory circulating in information technology (IT) security and compliance circles indicates that inadequate, spreadsheet-based internal controls may have played a part in allowing Société Générale's rogue trader Jerome Kerviel to build up positions that eventually resulted in a 7 billion euro loss for the bank. There has been some speculation that in addition to disguising his trades through a fictitious company and colleagues' accounts, he had been able to circumvent internal warning systems by opening and manipulating the Excel spreadsheet reports used by managers to monitor traders' activities.

CONCLUDING THOUGHTS

Each organization has to weigh its risk tolerance against the potential exposure and loss and then come to its own decision. Implementing even just a few of the guidelines will provide some level of control. In the long term, if desktop applications are left without scrutiny, my experience says that a lot of damage can be done by disbursing incorrect amounts and/or to incorrect payees, not to mention being a *breeding ground for fraud.*

7

TRAVEL AND ENTERTAINMENT FRAUD: NOT *ALL* YOUR EMPLOYEES ARE HONEST

You are probably wondering just how common travel and entertainment (T&E) fraud really is. To get an answer to that question, *Accounts Payable Now & Tomorrow* polled its readers and asked them about such frauds, instructing them to ignore small-dollar occurrences like a movie or drinks that were charged against policy.

While this is certainly not something to be overlooked, it is not in the same category as a large-dollar fraud. Even with these instructions, 38.03 percent of the respondents indicated that they had some T&E fraud in their organizations.

In its biannual 2006 *Report to the Nation,* the Association of Certified Fraud Examiners (ACFE) reports that expense reimbursement ranked second in terms of frequency, but it had the lowest median loss at $25,000. Fraud tends to be committed by long-term, trusted employees. Adding insult to injury, the average losses increase with tenure. Of course, some of this makes sense, as the longer the employee is with an organization, the longer he or she has to commit the fraud.

THE BOOK THAT TEACHES YOUR EMPLOYEES
HOW TO STEAL

Every time I give a lecture on fraud, I have this debate with myself over whether or not to mention the book that instructs your employees how to cheat on their T&E reports. I guess if there are books on how to make bombs, I shouldn't be too surprised about a book making the rounds entitled *How to Pad Your Expense Report ... and Get Away with It!* (Lubbock, TX: Easy Money Press, 1996).

It has been around for years, and some of the tactics the author recommends no longer work. However, many do, especially if you don't use an automated T&E system. Employee X (the author) provides tips to those who want to increase their income by illegally inflating their expense reports. I have read this slim book and made copious notes—on what companies can do to ensure that their employees do not employ the ruses suggested in this book. What follows is a look at some of the more egregious practices advocated, a list of signs you can look for on employee T&E reports that might signal a problem, and some recommended best practices.

DANGER SIGNS

Many of the strategies revolve around getting receipts. For example, employees booking airline trips themselves are advised to book several flights for the trip they will ultimately take. Once they have that coveted receipt for an expensive trip in hand, they can cancel that trip and book a less expensive one while submitting the receipt for the most expensive trip. Here are some of the things you should look for to help uncover possible fraud (and, yes, fraud is exactly what these strategies are):

- Sequential numbers on receipts, especially cash receipts. Compare several expense reports for the same employee if you suspect one.

- If there are more than occasional handwritten charge slips, take a closer look at the entire report.
- Too many cash receipts, especially if they look like adding machine tape, for low-cost meals.
- Double check the reports of employees traveling together to make sure that they are not both submitting for meal reimbursement for each other.
- Look really closely at the receipts for e-tickets. If you have the slightest doubt that the trip was taken, ask for the boarding passes. Of course, even this will not guard against the multiple-booking strategy discussed above.

Proceed carefully. Not everything that looks like a scam *is* a scam. Sometimes a handwritten receipt is legit. But a preponderance of these types of signs on one employee's reimbursement forms is generally a signal that further investigation is required. Let me point out something else: an employee who cheats regularly on his or her expense account is likely to have other problems. Many a corporate fraud has been uncovered because the individual involved got sloppy with expense reports.

OTHER T&E SCAMS

In addition to the airfare scheme discussed earlier, a similar strategy can be used at hotels. Employees entitled to lower room rates, perhaps because of a convention or corporate rate, neglect to mention this when checking in. Then, after they've checked out and gotten that all-important receipt, they return to the front desk, make a fuss, and get charged the lower rate. And then, of course, they hold on to that first coveted invoice showing the higher rate.

Similar scams involve ordering food service in a hotel and then complaining and having it taken off the bill, taking a friend instead of a business client to dinner (because your boss will never check up with the client), submitting group receipts where the group members have already reimbursed you, and so on.

DRAWING A LINE

Dumpster diving is another practice advocated to get those sought-after receipts! How far is Employee X willing to go? Here's what he says: "Failing the above methods, there is always the old standby of going through the trash." He goes on to note that no one watches the trash, which is unfortunate because this is where most crooks get credit card numbers. You'll be happy to know he does not condone this practice. He writes, "For some strange reason, I don't see anything morally wrong with ripping off my company through expense reports, but using someone else's charge card number is not fair to fellow travelers."

There's another dishonest aspect to his practices that he never addresses, either. Many of his techniques revolve around bullying or harassing the clerks who work in the hotels and restaurants. Telling the room service staff that the food was poor when you actually enjoyed the meal is despicable.

LATEST T&E ISSUE: VERIFYING BOARDING PASSES PRINTED AT HOME

Recently, for the first time, I printed out my boarding pass on my home computer before heading out to the airport for a business trip. A number of airlines have been using this method for some time, and it is a wonderful shortcut for those looking to avoid long check-in lines. In theory, this practice makes a lot of sense—unless the traveler needs to use the boarding pass for a business verification reason.

"So, what's the problem?," you ask. In the business world and the T&E environs, the boarding pass is used for more than airline business. To prove that a traveler has actually taken the trip for which he or she is asking reimbursement, many organizations require that the traveler submit a boarding pass. It occurs to me that if you can print it out on your computer at home, checking such boarding passes is worthless as a fraud deterrent or as a method of determining that the employee really took the trip.

The boarding pass could be printed and not used or, worse, easily altered. All but the most novice of today's professionals proficient with scanners and computers could easily modify the boarding pass to indicate whatever they wish.

The problem is twofold:

1. Determining whether the employee actually took the trip #20
2. Determining whether the employee actually took the flight indicated on the boarding pass or a less expensive one

SOLUTIONS TO THE BOARDING PASS ISSUE

If you are scratching your head, trying to figure out a solution to these emerging issues, you are not alone. When a conference is involved, there are partial solutions at hand. The most obvious: require the employee to turn in his or her conference badge. But that's not the only way to handle this particular part of the problem. Here's how Donna Robinson of College of the Sequoias solves the issue: "We always require something from the conference itself—preferably the agenda, or the cover of the book they receive when they check into the conference," she says. "It usually gives the name of the conference, location, and dates, and we compare that to the dates of travel claimed."

When the trip involves a customer visit or some other travel on company business, it is obvious that the above solutions won't work. And, frankly, we don't have a good recommendation here, although we suspect there is less cheating on this type of trip than when someone claims he or she is going to a conference and never leaves home.

The solution to the second issue is relatively straightforward. The only way an employee can gain from booking several flights and canceling all but the cheapest (while putting in for reimbursement for the most expensive) is if he or she uses a personal credit card. This type of fraud just doesn't work when using a company credit card, even if the employee is responsible for the payment. Thus, the answer here might simply be to insist on use of a company credit card.

It is unfortunate that a few bad apples make this type of checking necessary. Sadly, that's the world we live in today. Very few employees would have the nerve to put in for reimbursement for a trip never taken. But, alas, since a few do exist, it is necessary for accounts payable departments to go the extra mile and make sure everyone claiming conference attendance actually got there.

T&E FRAUD PREVENTION BEST PRACTICES

So, what can you do to ensure that none of your employees ask for reimbursements that they are not entitled to? Here are some suggestions:

- Have a firm policy, endorsed by upper management, that makes it clear to all employees that cheating on an expense report will result in termination. We're not talking about someone who makes a small honest mistake. We are talking about the guy who pays $178 for a plane ticket but manages to come up with a receipt for $673 and asks for reimbursement for the larger amount.
- Use a corporate T&E card. Until I read the book *How to Pad Your Expense Report . . . and Get Away with It!*, I didn't think it was crucial other than for financial cost-saving reasons. Any large company with more than a few employees leaves itself open to this type of fraud if they do not use one.
- If a corporate T&E card is not used, make it clear to employees that you have the right to see the credit card bills for the account they use for business events. When in doubt, ask for

the credit card bill in question and the one for the following month. Sometimes, the dubious refunds will not show up until the following month.

- While we do not advocate thoroughly checking every expense report, randomly select a certain percentage each month and verify every last cent on that report. Make sure your travelers know this is done.

- Should your suspicions be aroused regarding any one employee, put that individual's reports on the to-be-checked-thoroughly list each month.

- Once a year, select a small number of employees who travel a lot and pull all their reports. Look at them in total. Does anything strike you as odd? Are there sequentially numbered receipts?

- Periodically send a traveler a note that says, "Congratulations! You have successfully passed your expense reimbursement audit," and let the rumor mill take care of the rest. This puts your employees on notice that checking of expense reports is going on even if their bosses never give the reports a second glance.

DETECTING EXPENSE REIMBURSEMENT FRAUD

Your processors should be suspicious and have the right to ask for additional documentation if they suspect something is not right. They should have the right to ask anyone, right up to the president of the organization, and management should back them.

When spot checking expense reports, always check your known rogue spenders and make sure they know they are being monitored. Given the preceding statistics, always check your senior executives as well. Not only do they fall into the group more likely to commit expense reimbursement fraud, they also tend to spend the most money. This is a question of getting the most bang for your expense-review buck.

Your policy should require that the highest-ranking employee at an event pay for and submit for reimbursement when more than one employee is included in an event. Spot check your receipts closely when there is a large expenditure for entertainment to make sure that the manager approving the expense was not included in that entertainment.

Periodically, double check the mileage being submitted by travelers for reimbursement. Use one of the online mapping sites such as MapQuest. While the mileage won't be exact, it should be close.

UNIFORM ENFORCEMENT OF THE T&E POLICY

The saying "rank has its privileges" sets most employees' teeth grinding, especially when they see a high-level executive getting away with something that would not be tolerated by an employee at a lower level. It happens all the time at a significant number of organizations across the country. And, when it does, it sends employee morale tumbling and provides the rationalization to an employee looking to rip off his or her employer through T&E fraud.

Uniform policy enforcement is an issue every organization needs to evaluate if they truly want to stamp out T&E fraud. In an *Accounts Payable Now & Tomorrow* survey, 80 percent of the respondents indicated that the T&E policy was enforced uniformly in their organization, but that means there is a problem at 20 percent of the responding organizations. I got a good chuckle from the employee who very wisely responded anonymously, saying the policy was enforced uniformly in her organization—for everyone except the president! This is not setting a good example.

WHAT TO DO WHEN EXPENSE REIMBURSEMENT FRAUD IS DETECTED

There is no right or wrong way to deal with this issue. The organization should have a policy for dealing with employee fraud and decide in advance what it is. Then it should be applied uniformly. If it is not, the organization could be opening itself up to all sorts of discrimination claims. Most organizations will give the employee the opportunity to make reimbursement if the dollar amount is small and it is a one-time offense. They take the view that it is an honest mistake, and that may very well be the case. Others just don't take it seriously. This is a matter of corporate culture and varies greatly.

Take the example of two women caught submitting the same meal receipt from their first business trip. Most would just reprimand them, but their company took the position that fraud is fraud and fired the two. The benefit of this stance is that if it is public, it sets an example and serves as a deterrent to other employees. This does not mean that there needs to be an announcement, especially in the case of small dollars. However, by making sure that it is not kept a secret, most companies can rely on their ever-efficient rumor mill to get the word out.

The really unfortunate factor in the case of the two women discussed above is that if they hadn't owned up to the crime, but rather said it was a mistake, they probably would have saved their jobs. Their honesty after the fact hurt them.

The next issue revolves around whether to demand restitution and whether to prosecute. Even if restitution is demanded, few organizations ever get it, and even fewer get 100 percent of what is owed.

Prosecution is a delicate issue. Many simply let the employee go and eat the loss, avoiding getting the police involved. They do not wish the public scrutiny that prosecution could bring. Not prosecuting leaves the employee free to go elsewhere and commit similar crimes, especially if he or she is under pressure to make restitution of a serious amount of money.

LAST-DITCH COLLECTION EFFORTS

While most employees who are caught in expense reimbursement fraud will agree to make restitution, getting those funds often turns out to be a bigger problem than anticipated. Before implementing the following suggestion, make sure you have senior management approval in writing, for this is bound to bring some loud complaints.

If the person involved is still employed by the company and restitution seems to be unlikely, add the amount to the person's W-2 at year end, effectively turning it into taxable income. In a much publicized case involving the president of American University, the university was so outraged by his behavior that they retroactively corrected his W-2s for the amounts involved. More than one year was involved. The individual then had to deal with the IRS over taxes owed.

If the person involved is not employed by the company and restitution seems to be going nowhere, some have had success with reporting it on a 1099. If you use either of these approaches, make sure to discuss it with your tax professionals before taking action.

Perhaps just the threat of this might be enough to get the funds back.

FRAUD IN THE REAL WORLD

Here are some stories from readers and the newspapers illustrating the points made above. To my mind, some of them prove that life is indeed stranger than fiction.

- A frequent traveler was racking up *huge* entertainment expenses (dinners, etc.) and was allowed to get away with it for quite some time. I was directed to do some undercover investigating, such as getting detailed restaurant receipts instead of the grand total ones he submitted, to verify just how much, and for how many people, these dinners were. Eventually, he was made to reimburse the company for the apparent excess. It could have been avoided if daily meal limits had been imposed and adhered to.

- An employee purchased an audio course meant to be completed anywhere and made it look like a conference that he needed to attend so we would reimburse him for travel to Orlando (where he took his family). When this was caught we went back three years, and he had done the same thing about two years earlier. This was presented to his vice president, who called him on it and made him pay back the previous travel expenses over four payroll periods. This could have been prevented with closer review of reimbursement requests by management, human resources, and accounts payable.

- The employee in question was a salesperson working for two competing companies at the same time. She claimed the same travel expenses to both companies. When this was discovered, she was let go.

- Mileage was claimed for things such as attending an employee's family member's funeral, even though the funeral was during a day for which he was being paid. Mileage to every away sports event was claimed. Mileage to his own retirement party was claimed.

- Some of our T&E fraud detection comes from phone calls. The expense reports are pulled and audited over a six-month period. We have not switched to auditing our expense reports several at a time instead of one per person.

- Strong internal controls prevent most fraud, though T&E fraud is a different animal. It's hard for an employee to tell the "big boss" that an item on his expense report isn't appropriate, even when (true story) it's a $3,000 purse—and not for his wife!

- A salesperson who traveled extensively would come into accounts payable and ask to see his expense reports because he couldn't remember what he had submitted. This was before automation. He would actually remove receipts that he had submitted and submit them a second time. He got caught because one rang a bell with the processor who went back and discovered the missing receipt on the old report. This same person got a pad of prenumbered receipts that small diners use and stupidly submitted them in numerical order. He was fired, prosecuted, and went to jail.

- We had two employees who traveled together to a conference in Las Vegas, and each of them took a companion. When the expense reports were turned in, they included all their expenses for themselves and their companions. Another detail that was disturbing was their need for a rental car. Not necessary for the conference, but convenient for their personal excursions. We were able to catch this one prior to its being paid and the employees were written up and highly scrutinized for all future travel requests.

- An employee decided to modify a receipt to show a higher dollar amount than had actually been spent. Since the employee couldn't line up the numbers correctly, he or she used typewriter eraser tape and correction fluid to enter a new dollar amount. The receipts were scanned and e-mailed in. A really alert processor noticed a few minor odd-looking dashes on the scanned receipt and requested the original. Here comes what one of the professionals hearing this story dubbed "that special kind of stupid": the employee sent the original receipt—with all the correction fluid and tape—to the processor.

CLOSING THOUGHTS

The dollars involved in T&E frauds do not tend to be of the magnitude of other frauds, so some may think, "Why bother?" There are two reasons to bother. First, any fraud will grow if left undetected and unpunished. Second, many more advanced frauds have been uncovered because the crook got greedy and couldn't resist the lure of getting a few more dollars by cheating on T&E. The frauds came to light when the investigation of the T&E fraud was begun. This alone is reason enough to continually watch for T&E fraud.

8

PETTY CASH FRAUD: PETTY INDEED

Petty cash boxes were a staple of the corporate world when many places did not take credit cards and even fewer employees had corporate credit cards. Now, with places like McDonald's taking credit (or debit) cards for a hamburger and Starbucks and other java shops readily accepting cards, the need for a petty cash box has diminished and in some places is really nonexistent. In my opinion, few organizations have a true need for a petty cash box, and those that don't should get rid of them immediately. Operating a petty cash box is an extremely inefficient use of corporate human resources, especially when most organizations have cut staff right to the bone. What's more, the cash in the boxes is like a red flag in front of a bull to any employee who might be tempted to steal from you.

PETTY CASH AWFUL PRACTICES

Don't think I am making up the stuff in this section. I have seen all these practices in play, and I'm betting that most reading this have as well.

- Cashing personal checks in the box
- Accepting postdated personal checks in the box
- Accepting an IOU from an employee for cash in the box (In one instance the employee with the IOU had a heart attack and died with an outstanding IOU in his company's box.)

- Reimbursing employees for expenditures that should have been put on the travel and entertainment (T&E) report (but were outside policy!)
- Borrowing by the petty cash administrator without his putting an IOU in the box
- Keeping other valuables in the petty cash box

If I haven't convinced you yet not to have a petty cash box, let's talk about the controls you can put in place to prevent fraud.

HOW MUCH MONEY SHOULD THE BOX HAVE?

Assuming you are reading this because you have rejected the idea of no petty cash box, you will need to decide on the level of cash to have in the box. Start out by setting the level at 125 percent of the amount you expect to spend in one month. If that is $100, then start the box out with $125. Most organizations use a reimbursement approach referred to as an imprest. The approach is that you periodically top your cash box back up to a predefined level of cash—in our simple example, $125.

Whenever someone makes a payment from the cash box, a petty cash voucher is completed for exactly the same amount as the payment and put into the cash box. The voucher must be approved and a receipt attached to the voucher, if applicable. A register should be kept, showing the deductions. At any point in time, the remaining cash plus the approved vouchers should equal your original predefined amount. Notice that there was no mention of IOUs or third-party checks.

The box is reimbursed periodically, for an amount equal to the vouchers in the box. These vouchers can be used as backup for the disbursement request.

Companies sometimes get sloppy with this process. Often, you'll find a receipt in the box with an approval scrawled across it. This is the beginning of trouble. Once employees realize that any receipt with a scrawl on it can be used to get cash out of the box, a light goes off.

The other problem in this arena is the attention managers give to approving receipts for reimbursement. It is the same problem that occurs with T&E. Few managers actually take a close look at what they are signing. Thus, if you have a box, it must be emphasized that only genuine business-related expenses should be authorized. Source documentation such as receipts or invoices need to be shown to the person authorizing the expenditure. The approver should be held accountable in case of fraud.

While this example is for a very small petty cash box, it should be noted that many organizations keep thousands of dollars in their petty cash box. It is not uncommon to see a $20,000 predefined level in a box.

PETTY CASH BOX

The petty cash box should be a secure box with a lock and key. Don't keep it and the receipts in a big manila envelope in some-one's desk. That's just begging for trouble. Ideally, there would be one key to the box and only one person responsible. But that is not realistic, as people take vacations and have unexpected absences. There should only be two or three keys, and these should be given to people who will actually handle the petty cash disbursements. Too often, one or more senior executives insist on having the key. This is akin to making executives check signers who, in reality, will never see a check.

Many organizations place the locked petty cash box in a safe. The person with the combination to the safe is different than the person with the key to the petty cash box. Is this overkill? I don't think so. If the petty cash box is kept in an unlocked desk or file cabinet, anyone can steal the box and break it open once they get it away. While it is unlikely anyone would go to this trouble for a $125 box, they might for a box with $20,000 in it.

The person assigned responsibility for the petty cash box needs to understand who can approve payments and should keep a register. At any given point, the cash in the box plus approved receipts should equal the amount.

SURPRISE AUDITS

From time to time, a manager should perform a spot check on the petty cash box and the records. These surprise audits should verify that:

- Vouchers are signed, with supporting documentation attached.
- The cash is regularly counted and the balance reconciled to the petty cash records.
- Wages are not being paid from petty cash.
- The staff is not borrowing from petty cash.
- If you are in a business that gets paid with cash, any cash is kept separately in an income cash box and not mixed with petty cash. While it might be tempting to reimburse the petty cash box from your cash register, resist the temptation.

WHERE DOES RESPONSIBILITY FOR THE BOX LIE?

Petty cash is one of those annoying responsibilities that no one wants. It can be in:

- Treasury
- Accounts payable
- Human resources
- Accounting (other than accounts payable)

It does not really matter where the function lies as long as the professional handling it takes the issue seriously and is not sloppy. Of course, it goes without saying that segregation-of-duties issues should be addressed. No one should have the authority to approve a voucher and then reimburse himself out of the box. Someone independent of the custodian should be replenishing this fund, reviewing supporting documentation, and conducting surprise audits of petty cash.

When the surprise audit is conducted, there should be two parties present when the cash is counted. This control will prevent finger pointing should it turn out that the box is short the cash it is supposed to have.

DO WE STILL NEED PETTY CASH?

From time to time, say every two years, organizations that have a petty cash box should evaluate whether they really need one. How much money has been reimbursed through the box? Is it small enough that it would not be unreasonable to ask executives to pay for it themselves and then seek reimbursement on their T&E? Organizations that give employees corporate procurement cards may find that they no longer need a petty cash box either.

Many times organizations have these boxes because of the corporate culture. The culture in the organization is such that management does not like to ask employees to put out their own funds for the company's benefit, even if it is only for a few days. Weigh the value of this against the cost of running the box and the fraud risk. Most have decided to forgo the box.

RECEIPT REVIEW

From time to time, someone from internal audit, your external auditors, or accounting should take all the receipts used for reimbursement from the petty cash box and look at them. Ideally, nothing will emerge. However, you may find:

- The same receipt used numerous times

- One individual putting in numerous times for something that is purchased once a year or very infrequently
- A disturbing number of what look like personal receipts
- Receipts from a prenumbered pad in numerical order
- Anything else that looks fishy

Often, a single receipt may not look out of place, but when taken as part of a bigger picture, it becomes apparent that something is rotten in Denmark.

This is not a task you would undertake for a very small box. But, if the box disburses $10,000 or $20,000 or more a month, you might want to do a little investigating. While you are at it, determine if there is a better way to pay for some of these things.

PETTY CASH VERSUS T&E

Never reimburse something from the petty cash box that should have been put on an employee's T&E reimbursement form. Insist that it go on the T&E. Otherwise, you find an employee double dipping— requesting reimbursement for the same item from both pots.

FRAUD IN THE REAL WORLD

Here are some stories from readers and the newspapers illustrating the points made above. To my mind, some of them prove that life is indeed stranger than fiction.

- A university employee stole more than $20,000 from the university's petty cash fund by submitting fraudulent receipts.
- A college accountant in the dean's office forged signatures on vouchers, stealing over $6,500 over a period of two years.

CONCLUDING THOUGHTS

How strong are the controls that govern this area in your organization? Many companies rationalize this area as being immaterial. We've all heard that there is no level of immateriality on fraud or theft. Expenditures should be well documented with the original receipts from the individuals requiring reimbursement.

9

VENDOR AND INVOICE FRAUD: NOT EVERY INVOICE (OR VENDOR!) IS LEGIT

Unfortunately, there are many individuals who would rather spend their time trying to bilk honest organizations out of their money than putting in an honest day's work. These crooks capitalize on the knowledge that accounts payable departments are overworked and do not usually have the resources to devote adequate attention to small-dollar invoices. Sometimes they will deliver shoddy or low-quality goods to a company, and these companies bill them for those products at inflated prices. A few of the more outrageous thieves will even try to aggressively collect on these invoices. The most common schemes involve copier paper, toner for copy machines, help wanted advertisements, and yellow pages ads.

Some of these invoices will fall into the category of no purchase order (PO) number, no requisitioner, with good reason—no one ordered the goods. That's why a "no PO, no check" policy works well. It stops these guys in their tracks.

Insisting on a PO for all goods is another way to eliminate these invoices from phantom vendors.

Now, if you are thinking that it is no big deal for most organizations if they pay a $25 invoice that is fraudulent, you are both right and wrong. While the bottom-line impact of that one invoice is small, there are bigger implications. Few fraudulent vendors willingly walk away from a gravy train. The company that pays one invoice will receive additional ones.

Good up-front vendor verification programs will also help nip this problem in the bud.

FRAUDULENT INVOICES—OR NOT

With certain invoices, it is very easy to tell they are fraudulent. They represent goods never ordered from vendors you've never done business with. Others are not so clear. Is it a fraudulent invoice, or did the vendor make an honest mistake? For example, if the invoice includes:

- Extravagant terms
- Inflated prices
- Including charges not agreed to
- Amounts higher than ordered
- Amounts larger than delivered

you need to tread very carefully. The errors could arise from a misunderstanding or a sloppy employee, or the vendor could be purposely trying to get you to pay for more than you ordered. If this happens on rare occasions, treat it as an honest mistake. If it happens regularly, you need to decide whether this is some-one you want to do business with on a long-term basis. It doesn't really matter if it's fraud or sloppiness. If the vendor can't get its billing act together, you can either make up your mind to go over every invoice from that vendor very carefully, or you can take your business elsewhere.

SOLICITATIONS THAT LOOK LIKE INVOICES

One of the most common variations of the phony invoice scheme is issuing solicitations disguised as invoices. These documents, which are actually solicitations for the purchase of goods or services, are carefully designed to look like legitimate invoices for goods or services ordered and received. Often, they are for legal or regulatory products, and you may even think you are paying for a required filing fee. However, upon close inspection of the document, it will become clear that it is not an invoice. The trick here is to inspect the document closely because, having seen some, I can tell you they are quite good.

What can you do? Just be aware that this is going on and scrutinize everything that comes in. One of the reasons these scams work is that, in general, they are for a relatively low dollar amount, so most organizations don't bother checking thoroughly. This is unfortunate because the Better Business Bureau reports that many of these phony invoices do indeed get paid. And, while I have no inside knowledge of this, I have to believe that once you pay a phony invoice, the crooks try your name on another of their lists.

OTHER COMMON INVOICE FRAUDS

Another approach taken by enterprising crooks looking to get their hands on a few of your dollars is to emulate legitimate orders you did place. The two favorite places they do this are yellow pages ads and help wanted ads. Some will even attach a tear sheet that looks exactly like the order you did indeed place. Only when you look closely will you see that the entity that is billing you is not the one where you placed your ad. And, if you pay the phony invoice, you will still owe the legitimate vendor for the services provided.

Some do actually publish a product with your ad, so if you pay, you might say that technically it is not fraud—if you overlook the fact that you never placed an order with the entity. With more help wanted advertising moving to the Internet, it is likely that this type of invoice fraud will disappear. But the yellow pages fraud will remain.

There is also a version of the yellow pages fraud that sends along what is technically called a billing notice, not an invoice asking for payment for an ad.

FRAUD AND POOR PAYMENT PRACTICES

Let's take a step back for a moment and look at what happens when invoices don't get paid on time, regardless of the reason. After 30 days, most vendors will send a second invoice. Some will mark the invoice "duplicate," "copy," or "second notice," and some won't. A few will actually give that second invoice a different invoice number (more on that later). When the second invoice shows up, many get approved and sent down to accounts payable for payment.

In fact, in some cases, for reasons that are beyond comprehension, the second invoice arrives first. Depending on how stringent the coding standards and procedural practices are in accounts payable, that second invoice may or may not get paid. This is one reason why we emphasize that controls put in to prevent fraud also help reduce duplicate payments and vice versa.

Now, what happens occasionally is that a vendor gets fed up and calls accounts payable, demanding payment. Depending on everything that has gone on with regard to this particular invoice, the vendor's history with the customer in general, and the vendor's temperament, the vendor may lose his or her cool and start screaming. Many will threaten to put the account on credit hold. For many accounts payable departments, this is a fate worse than death—especially if the vendor in question is supplying a key ingredient to their manufacturing process. One vendor could hypothetically shut down the whole manufacturing plant. And, believe me when I tell you, no one in accounts payable wants to be responsible for that!

So, vendors who are fed up and want to be paid will scream, threatening credit hold. So will some who just want to be paid faster. And, lo and behold, crooks have figured this game out as well and know if they call accounts payable and start screaming, they are likely to get paid with a rush manual check immediately—and that is just what they want. What has emerged is that the largest numbers of fraudulent checks are:

- Issued to screaming vendors
- Rush checks
- Returned to requisitioners

Here's a true story. It happened at a Fortune 500 company, one everyone reading this would recognize. It has a top-notch accounts payable process, pays everyone on time, and generally has few vendor problems. One day, one of the processors came to the accounts payable director in tears. She'd just gotten off the phone with a consultant used by one of the company's subsidiaries. She apparently had had rows with him every month. He claimed at the top of his lungs that it would be easier "to get a rooster to lay an egg on a picket fence in New York City in July than to get paid on time" by the company in question. The director saw stars.

She instructed the processor to pull all payments to this consultant for the last two years. They discovered that he had been playing this game every month, successfully bullying duplicate payments from the organization to the tune of $300,000. The company requested that the consultant come in for a meeting and then ambushed him with the payment data. He lost the consulting assignment and had to repay the company.

He knew about the screaming game. Now you do, too. Treat every screamer with an extreme amount of caution.

By the way—not that this really has anything to do with fraud, but this is part of the reason I am very much against stretching payments unless there is a cash flow problem—if your controls aren't iron tight, you will end up duplicate paying one or more vendors, giving back all the savings you were supposed to get from your stretching program.

A WORD ABOUT COLLUSION

One of the reasons that we talk so much about segregation of duties is that it is much less likely a fraud will be committed if you need two people to work together to commit the crime. One will either have an ethical issue with the fraud or just be plain chicken. Thus, by taking the appropriate steps, you can make it less likely that fraud will be committed against your organization.

However, when one of your employees gets in cahoots with an employee at one of your suppliers, you are less likely to be able to figure it out. If a vendor sends what looks like a legitimate invoice to your purchasing manager and he or she approves it, the payment will likely get made. If you are thinking the purchasing manager could send the invoice without having a legitimate vendor on the other end of the transaction, you are correct. It is one of the reasons the three-way match (invoice against PO and receiving document) is critical.

There are other issues to be concerned about. The legitimate vendor could send an invoice for 100 widgets, shipping 50 to your organization and 50 to your purchasing manager. How would you catch this? By having a top-flight receiving staff. This does not always happen. In quite a few organizations, the receiving documents are checked off without a close inspection of what was actually received. Hence, it is critical that receiving do a thorough check before signing off on receiving documents.

BRIEF COMMENTARY ON PURCHASING

Since we alluded to purchasing fraud, we'll touch on it briefly. Every organization should have a written purchasing policy, spelling out a code of conduct for its employees who spend on behalf of the organization. Many organizations have a strict $25 limit on the value of gifts their employees can accept. This is a good practice, and it should be followed right down the line.

It can be very hard for an executive who is getting football tickets every Sunday to make an impartial decision. Similarly, big gifts delivered to the employee's home or spouse need to be expressly forbidden. Accepting such gifts should be a firing offense. While these practices are less common today than they were 20 years ago, there are still vendors who will try. By being aware of these practices and making your employees aware of the consequences of accepting such gifts, you will have gone a long way to putting an end to this type of manipulation of your staff.

UP-FRONT VENDOR VERIFICATION

Along with proper internal controls and segregation of duties, establishing proper controls when adding a new vendor or updating the master vendor file will reduce your exposure to fraud. Without being complacent regarding fraud, you are probably comfortable with your current updating process. However, many accounts payable shops are faced with recent or anticipated accounts payable system and process changes. Inevitably, these disrupt the master vendor process status quo. To gain increased efficiencies and productivity, accounts payable and procurement applications rely on the use of Internet and intranet technologies to update the master vendor. Use of these technologies actually presents an opportunity for accounts payable to improve internal controls and, at the same time, may present internal control challenges when the master vendor file is updated. (Pinpoint Profit Recovery Services' Bob Lovallo provided the intelligence for this up-front vendor verification section.)

CONTROL CHALLENGE IN REAL LIFE

Despite significant investment in internal corporate controls in the wake of the Sarbanes-Oxley Act, according to a recent global study by PricewaterhouseCoopers and Martin Luther University in Germany, corporate fraud has increased 22 percent over the past two years. The study also noted that most corporate fraud was detected by accidental means. Therefore, implementing preemptive internal control enhancements will only help in your attempt to minimize your exposure to fraud, especially when the integrity of the master vendor file is to be maintained.

During a recent client recovery audit Lovallo worked on, accounts payable head count was reduced when the company installed an accounts payable–linked front-end intranet application. The new process allowed and authorized non–accounts payable employees to enter invoice and account code data as well as access the master vendor file to identify the vendor number and so forth. The data was edited for completeness and for valid account coding before it reached the accounts payable application and accounts payable processor.

When the invoice and the approved input document were received in accounts payable, the processor would perform his or her normal processing and approval routines. What caught Lovallo's attention was that the process now allowed employees who performed the front-end invoice processing to establish a new vendor in the master vendor file. Although the new vendor had to be approved by an independent party, he believed the new process opened up accounts payable to potential employee mischief and fraudsters. Although accounts payable increased its vigilance over the new process, some additional actions using the Internet to guard against potential fraud involving the master vendor file needed to be taken.

What follows is a look at some of Lovallo's recommendations to limit the potential for vendor/employee fraud related to establishing a vendor.

Who Is Confirmed

First, verify that new vendors with significant first-time payments are legit. Also check payments to vendors who provide only a post office box as a "remit to" or address. Use Dun & Bradstreet (D&B)

and other manual means to confirm authenticity, such as the yellow pages, phone contact, and so forth. Today, it is much easier to perform this check on almost every new vendor using the Internet to check yellow pages, run Google searches, and access sites such as D&B and Hoover's. During audits, Lovallo always recommends this added control to protect his clients against potential fraud.

Why Front-End Verification Is Important

Since there are a number of frond-end accounts payable systems, he believes this is important. For example, the employee prints out the cover sheet, obtains management approval (signatures) on the cover sheet, attaches the invoice to the cover sheet, and forwards the packet to accounts payable for payment. In such front-end systems where every field must be completed by the invoice submitter, mischief can occur.

Therefore, Lovallo believes it is critical to have vendor verification to prevent fraud when new vendors can be added by employees or even other company-assigned employees. You may want to address this by adding another separate vendor verification control point.

New Vendor Verification Guidelines

He highly recommends that someone not directly involved in setting up the vendor entry perform a double check. Any vendor who submits a post office box for an address and no telephone number deserves a little additional scrutiny. Many organizations do not have the staff to verify every new vendor, so the list below can be used by your staff when selecting new vendors to verify:

- Vendors whose invoices do not have invoice numbers
- Vendors with post office box addresses
- Any new vendor over a certain dollar amount
- Hand-typed invoices

- Any new invoice that looks odd
- A certain percentage of all new vendors

When verifying a new vendor, one of the first places to check is the yellow pages. Not every legitimate vendor advertises there. In fact, depending on your business, you will find that many don't, so be sure to use the online resources discussed earlier.

During your cross-checking, keep a record of where you found the verification information. Each company will need to select the criteria that they want to check, the items that they think will protect them the best.

One Last Technique

Even if you don't actually verify vendors in accounts payable, you can tell people that you do. Put a little blurb on your material saying that "New vendors set up outside accounts payable will be verified by accounts payable." This warning will help scare off petty theft. The unscrupulous will have to be a little more creative if they want to defraud your organization.

Similarly, you can create a long list of items verified—even if you don't check everything. This is one place where it is perfectly acceptable for accounts payable to be less than 100 percent honest. With limited staff, a little creative license is sometimes called for.

What this does is to help protect against collusion within the process since, ideally, the person checking in accounts payable is not the person who sets up the master vendor list. If your organization does not do this, it is being exposed to fraud, as vendor theft is among the easiest to commit.

Concluding Thoughts on Vendor Verification

Clearly, continued monitoring of the process will assess the quality of internal controls over time. Use of the Internet is cost effective and provides an opportunity to monitor the master vendor file updating process. Keep in mind that the extent of the controls adopted by any business is often limited by cost considerations. Realizing that it is not feasible from a cost standpoint to establish controls that provide 100 percent protection against fraud, adopting a vendor verification process will add reasonable assurances against fraud—and that's probably the best that can be achieved.

ADVICE FROM THE BETTER BUSINESS BUREAU

Recognizing that phony invoices are problematic for organizations of all sizes, the Better Business Bureau came up with the following guidelines. Use as many as you can.

- Never place an order over the telephone, unless there is no doubt that the firm you are dealing with is reputable. Get the organization's name, address, and phone number, as well as its representative's full name and position.
- If a significant amount of money is involved, ask for business and local bank references and check them. Find out how long the firm has operated out of its present location. If possible, visit the company or firm. Ask your local Better Business Bureau for a reliability report.
- Check your records to confirm claims of previous business dealings.
- Before placing advertising, make sure the publication exists. Verify its circulation figures and that its circulation suits your needs.
- Establish effective internal controls for the payment of invoices.
- Channel all bills through one department.
- Insist that employees fill out prenumbered purchase orders for every order placed.
- Check all invoices against purchase orders and against goods or services received. Make certain that order numbers correspond with the invoices.

- Verify all invoices with the person who gave written or verbal authorization.
- Clear all invoices with the appropriate executives.
- If the invoicing company claims to have a tape recording of the order, insist on hearing it.

FRAUD IN THE REAL WORLD

Here are some stories from readers and the newspapers illustrating the points made above. To my mind some of them prove that life is indeed stranger than fiction.

- We received an invoice, along with every hospital in South Dakota, that charged us for repairs on the furnace done on Christmas Eve. We've also received bills for advertisements that we did not place in magazines.
- We recently conducted a duplicate-payment audit for a small, health product–manufacturing firm. During the course of the audit, we noticed several checks without an invoice number. We had to use the check register as our base file, instead of an extract from the accounts payable file, which turned out to be a blessing: the checks without invoice numbers were in some cases fraudulent. We found a situation where one employee wrote four to five checks over $40,000 each to himself, without an invoice number. These invoices may not have been in the accounts payable system, because a system usually requires an invoice number. But, since we read the check register file (electronic copy of a report), we found these invoices! My advice would be to review the check register and reconcile it with the accounts payable system if not already done, or just do a quick check on invoices without invoice numbers.

CONCLUDING THOUGHTS

Clearly, both the invoices you receive and the vendors that send them provide an opportunity for those with thievery in their hearts. Thus, it is crucial that you take steps to guard against fraud in both those arenas. In Chapter 10 we will investigate master vendor file manipulations. Taking the right steps in that arena will help guard against vendor and invoice fraud.

10

MASTER VENDOR FILE FRAUD: HOW EMPLOYEES PLAY GAMES WITH YOUR RECORDS

The master vendor file and the policies and practices surrounding it, along with appropriate controls (or lack thereof), are one of the arcane areas in the procure-to-pay cycle that many don't understand, and an even greater number don't realize how poor controls can help internal fraudsters get access to your organization's money. If you are tempted to skip this section, please don't. It affects everyone reading this book.

The master vendor file is the repository of information for all vendors that the company does business with. Not just any vendor should be able to get into your master vendor file. Before a vendor is entered, information should be checked, verifying that the vendor is legitimate and that your organization intends to do business with it. Generally speaking, most organizations do not enter one-time vendors into their master vendor file. Controls around the information, both the initial data and any changes, should be strong.

This is an area that should not be overlooked when it comes to segregation of duties. If it is not apparent why, read on. The setting up of a vendor is the first step in many organizations to getting someone paid. Ideally, that someone is a vendor who has a legitimate right to be in your master vendor file.

Similarly, changes to the master vendor file should be guarded with the same care. Here's why. A crooked employee, realizing a big check was going out to ABC vendor, could go into the master vendor file, change the address in the file, and wait for you to issue the very legitimate check, sign it, and mail it. Once the check was mailed, the crafty employee could go back into your system and change the address back to the correct one.

SOME REALLY BAD MASTER VENDOR FILE PRACTICES

Since some organizations don't take the master vendor file into consideration when worrying about internal controls, some really awful practices are in place at a few organizations. Here's a list of some you should avoid—at all costs!

- Not limiting access of who can make changes or additions to the master vendor file
- Adding vendors to the master vendor file just because an invoice shows up from that vendor
- Having multiple parties enter information using no coding standards

- Letting someone approve invoices and enter information into the master vendor file

MASTER VENDOR FILE REPORTS

This is a recommendation that most controllers and chief financial officers (CFOs) hate. Once a month or once a week, depending on the level of activity in your accounts, a report should be run showing all activity in the master vendor file. It should include:

- All new vendors
- All changes of address
- Any other changes

This report should be reviewed. Now, here comes the part the controllers and CFOs generally don't like. It should be reviewed by a high-level executive, usually the controller or the CFO. Why? Because everyone on staff should know that the organization takes this matter seriously and that fooling around with the master vendor file is a firing offense.

In reality, I recognize that few controllers or CFOs have the time to do the review necessary. They can delegate it to a trusted staffer (who does not have access to add or make changes to the file) and only occasionally do the review themselves. If there is a question, the staffer doing the review should take it to the CFO, and he or she should be the one to make the inquiry into the problem. This is a case where the monitoring and reviewing is mostly a case of saber rattling so that everyone knows they cannot fool around with the master vendor file. If they want to try and steal from the company, they will have to find another way.

CODING STANDARDS PREVENT FRAUD

One of the common problems with the master vendor file is that organizations end up having the same vendor in it numerous times. This happens when strict coding standards are not used by everyone who makes entries or changes to the master vendor file. These coding standards refer to how vendors' names are entered, if and how abbreviations are entered (St. James Co. or Saint James Company), how leading articles are entered (*The New York Times* or *New York Times*), how individuals' names are entered (Mary Schaeffer or Schaeffer, Mary), and more.

Each organization needs to come up with a coding standard that works for it. In many instances there is no right or wrong way to do things. Whether you enter Mary Schaeffer or Schaeffer, Mary really doesn't matter—as long as everyone does it the same way. These standards can be quite complicated and should be given to everyone who makes entries. For a variety of other best-practice reasons, the standards or naming conventions used with the master vendor file should match the coding standards used by your invoice processors. There are samples in some accounts payable books or you can develop your own.

There is no one right standard. However, it is important to establish a standard that is consistently used by everyone who processes invoices and makes changes or enters new data in the master vendor file.

The reason excess vendors in the master vendor file are a problem is that your employees who wish to steal from you through invoice fraud will use one of the inactive vendors for the appropriate coding. Thus, it is important that the coding standard be used and there be only one entry per vendor in the master vendor file.

CLEANSING THE MASTER VENDOR FILE

As implied in the preceding section, excess entries in the master vendor file can provide refuge for an employee looking to steal by using phony invoices. Thus, it is important that inactive vendors be cleansed out of the master vendor file or deactivated. *Note:* it is important that the information not be deleted, as it may be needed at a future date.

Ideally, organizations would review their master vendor file once a year and deactivate or remove any vendor that had not been used within the last year, taking care to preserve the information. This does not always happen. In fact, most companies that do cleanse their master vendor file do so once every two years, and many never do it. That's right; they have vendors in the file that go back to the year of the flood.

If you have never cleansed the file, bite the bullet and get started. Most organizations do it at a slow time of the year for the accounts payable staff—or perhaps I should say the least hectic. For many that do not have a June 30 year end, the best time is the summer.

The first time the master vendor file is cleansed, it can be ugly. Some hire an outside service to help them, and others simply bite the bullet and download everything into an Excel spreadsheet and get started. The data has to be reviewed by someone who knows what they and you are doing.

If there are vendors in the file with duplicate entries, the activity in the accounts should be combined before all but one of the files is deactivated. Some accounting packages have a module that will help do this. I am not going to try and tell you this is an easy task—it is not. However, the difficulty comes not from the complexity of the task but the need to sort through the data manually.

It is a task that should be done regularly and, ideally, at least once a year. There are some progressive organizations that do a portion of their file every month. This keeps the project from becoming overwhelming and gets the file cleaned up.

If you have never done this before, consider hiring outside help to assist you. This can be as simple as a temp or use one of the third-party services available. It is too important to continue to ignore if you have never cleansed your files.

WHO HAS RESPONSIBILITY FOR THE MASTER VENDOR FILE

This can be a sore issue. It is sometimes in purchasing and sometimes in accounts payable. Remember, there has to be appropriate segregation of duties or the opportunity for fraud will skyrocket. The person who adds vendors to the master vendor file should not process invoices or have the ability to approve invoices or sign checks. In smaller accounts payable departments, the segregation-of-duties requirements make it impossible to have the master vendor file in the department.

Along the same lines, many in purchasing approve invoices for payment. Because of the segregation-of-duties requirements, they should not have access to the master vendor file.

Thus, some organizations put it in another accounting area, achieving the segregation-of-duties goals.

A NEW SYSTEM

It seems that the master vendor file issue raises its ugly head most frequently when there is a system conversion. The question usually goes something like this: "We know our master vendor file is a mess and we probably should have done something about it years ago, but we didn't. We're converting to a new system, and we wonder what we should do about the vendor file. The project manager says we really have too many vendors to transfer."

These organizations have three choices:

1. To transfer everything as is
2. To transfer nothing and start over, this time the right way
3. To cleanse the file and transfer the cleansed file

It is strongly recommended that the last approach be the one that is taken. Usually, it is known months, if not years, in advance that the system conversion is coming. Take that opportunity to start fresh with the best data. It is usually a time when it is slightly easier to get money for temps, so why not bite the bullet and start the right way with the new system?

If you take either of the other two approaches, you could be asking for trouble. By not transferring anything and asking all vendors for new information, the odds are extremely high that you will aggravate at least a few of your vendors. Plus, you will spend a lot of time entering the new information. Why not spend that time cleaning up your existing information. Plus, you run the risk of losing some of your historical data if you don't transfer the information and that could cause you problems later on.

If you take the other approach of transferring everything, you continue with bad habits, making it easy for your employees to use your vendor files to steal from you. And the risk of duplicate payments continues.

MASTER VENDOR FILE AND YOUR EMPLOYEES

Here's a check that should be done at least once a year. There's no need for anyone to know it is being done. Usually, the controller will have someone in information technology (IT) perform the task. Take the employees' address register from human resources and run it against the addresses in the master vendor file. Eliminate any matches that are a result of having the employees in the master vendor file for travel and entertainment (T&E) reimbursement purposes.

Review carefully any matches. The reason for this is simple. Many crooks are lazy, so they'll set up an invoice scheme and then have the checks mailed to their homes rather than set up a separate post office box. This certainly won't catch all employee invoice schemes, but it will help you detect a surprisingly large number of them, should they exist.

The suggestion of reviewing the matches carefully is because there could be legitimate matches, and it is crucial that no one is accused incorrectly. This run should be repeated each year, and, hopefully, you will never get a hit.

FRAUD IN THE REAL WORLD

Here are some stories from readers and the newspapers illustrating the points made above. To my mind, some of them prove that life is indeed stranger than fiction.

- An employee at a remote location submitted invoices for which there was no actual vendor, and then he pocketed the money. When discovered, he was fired. I took over accounts payable just after this and got control of the master vendor files (every vendor checked for existence) and had all invoices mailed directly to accounts payable instead of to the project managers. By manipulating the master vendor file and having invoices come directly to him, this employee was able to defraud the company over a period of years.

- We had an employee who had the ability to request vendor adds to the master vendor file. She also approved invoices, clearly inappropriate from a segregation-of-duties standpoint. She requested a fraudulent vendor setup and created invoices to be paid with her approval. She used a general ledger account that had a lot of activity and was not cost center relevant. Over several years she submitted thousands of dollars' worth of invoices. The fraud was identified through the anonymous hotline. It really opened my eyes to controls over the vendor master file. We now do extensive research prior to setting up a vendor.

CLOSING THOUGHTS

If you've never given your master vendor file a thought when it comes to fraud prevention, take a look at your practices and get them in line, with appropriate segregation of duties and internal controls. If the file has never been cleansed, make that a top priority, remembering to deactivate vendors who are inactive. Do not delete them or you will lose valuable historical information. Most accounting packages will allow this.

11

PAYROLL FRAUD: GHOSTBUSTING AND MORE

When the topic of payroll fraud is raised, most people think of phantom or ghost employees. And they are definitely part of the problem. Some think phantom employees are a problem mostly on construction jobs and the like, so it is not an issue they need to be concerned about. Those who believe this are, unfortunately, wrong on all fronts. Phantom employees have been found on the books of all sorts of organizations. And, as you will read in this chapter, it is not the only type of payroll fraud.

PHANTOM EMPLOYEES

Adding a fictitious person to the payroll and then collecting his or her paycheck on a regular basis is a nice way to supplement your income without having to lift a finger. Ghost employees are people on the payroll who don't actually work for the company. They can be living or dead. It doesn't really matter, since they will never see the paycheck with their name on it.

The phantom employee may be a recently departed employee, whom the payroll processor "forgot" to take off the payroll; a made-up person; or a friend or relative of the fraudster, who can cash the paycheck by forging the endorsement. If an accomplice is used, the accomplice deposits the proceeds into his or her bank account and then shares the profits.

Now, if you are wondering where the Social Security number comes from for these phony employees, the answer to that question is simple. The crook simply gets online, checks the death register, and picks a Social Security number that way. If they want to be consistent, although few do, they match the name with the correct Social Security number.

As for cashing the check, it is not a problem. If the name is completely different, they simply endorse it over to themselves. Some savvy crooks don't even bother with this process. They sign the phantom employee up for direct deposit. If they are lazy, they simply have the funds go to their own account. The more industrious have it go to another account so you won't find it when you have your information technology (IT) department do a check to see if more than one payroll check is being deposited to the same account.

WHAT YOU CAN DO TO DETECT AND PREVENT GHOST EMPLOYEES

This cannot be said enough: the proper segregation of duties when it comes to payroll is your first defense against payroll fraud. Make sure your payroll preparation, disbursement, and distribution functions are segregated.

Although it is not legal in all states, if it is in your state, mandating direct deposit of payroll makes it more difficult, although not impossible, to add fictitious employees to the payroll. Some brazen thieves using their own bank account will be uncovered when it comes to light that two employees are using the same bank account.

Crooks are greedy and often lazy. Look for paychecks without deductions for taxes or Social Security. Why should the crook pay taxes, although the smarter ones do. They don't want to add tax evasion to their list of crimes, should they be caught.

Some low-tech ways of uncovering phantom employees include the following:

- Examine payroll checks with dual endorsements. Although most of them are legitimate, two signatures could signal a forgery, with the fraudster also endorsing and depositing the check into his or her own account.
- Occasionally, have paychecks hand-delivered to employees and require positive identification, such as a driver's license. Verify that any remaining paychecks belong to actual employees, not phantom employees. This delivery should be unannounced.
- Each pay period, print a list of employees added to the payroll in that period and have a person not responsible for initiating new employees in the payroll confirm those names with the employee's supervisor.
- Periodically review payroll records for the presence of duplicate names, addresses, and Social Security numbers. Also, look at the direct deposit information to make sure that only one payroll check is being deposited into each account. Dual deposits should raise a red flag.

Don't overlook some of the more commonsense ways to prevent payroll fraud. Requiring payroll employees to take their vacations over the time when payroll is submitted and checks are distributed might be an inconvenience, but it will help uncover a fraud if one is going on.

Require the changing of passwords frequently. This will limit the damage caused by someone who has managed to get a password through illicit means.

FALSIFIED HOURS AND/OR SALARY

Another scheme used by those looking to increase their paychecks is to get paid for more hours than they worked or to manage to have their salary raised by someone with access to the payroll system. We are all familiar with the scam where one worker has another punch in or out for him so it looks like they worked longer hours.

Occasionally, crooked payroll associates will know of an internal control weakness that will permit them to adjust their own salaries and they take advantage of it. Remember, it is your employees who work intimately with your systems who are best aware of where the loopholes are. Anyone with access to the payroll system can manipulate the rates of pay or the hours worked. There have been occasions where these crooked employees not only gave themselves a raise but also gave themselves a bonus while they were at it. This is why it is critical that access be given only to those who absolutely need it to perform their jobs.

At some companies there is the belief that every vice president (or executive over a certain level) should have access. This just opens the door to trouble. Restrict access to only those who absolutely must have it.

And then there are the few supervisors who sometimes, for a share of the loot, approve an employee's falsified hours.

WHAT YOU CAN DO TO DETECT AND PREVENT EMPLOYEES FROM FALSIFYING DATA

To prevent payroll department employees from playing around with the data, require mandatory vacations for those with payroll responsibilities, with another employee performing this function in their absence. If they are changing data every pay period, it may come to light during this time period. Similarly, you can require an executive to approve all paychecks and any excess bonus-type compensation.

The issue with managers approving time cards is similar to managers approving travel and entertainment reimbursement requests. Many simply sign what is put in front of them without verifying that the data is accurate. Management must make managers aware that they are responsible for what they are signing, and there need to be some consequences for those who sign fraudulent time sheets, even if they are not in collusion. It's the only way to get people to pay attention to this responsibility.

Once again, the proper segregation of duties and tight controls around the payroll function will make it harder for employees to play games with the payroll.

Finally, technology can play a role, especially for those employees who punch a time clock. Some of the more sophisticated time clocks or systems require a unique employee pass code to be entered when clocking in and out. This makes it more difficult, although not impossible, for one employee to punch a whole group of employees in or out.

The most sophisticated of time clocks now incorporate a fingerprint scanner into the company's time clock. This makes it impossible for anyone but the employee to punch himself in or out.

COMMISSION SCHEMES

Salespeople and other employees working on commission can sometimes fallaciously increase their pay. These schemes generally fall into two categories:

35

1. Employees who find a way to falsify the amount of sales
2. Employees who find a way to increase their commission rate

The key for our readers is to ensure adequate controls to prevent the reporting of inaccurate data that will result in fraudulent payments to these employees.

Employees who find ways to report larger sales do it in a number of creative ways. They may:

- Report sales without reporting any subsequent credits.
- Knowingly make sales to entities with poor credit standing that turn into bad debts.
- Find ways to hide returns.

As an aside, although this has nothing to do with fraud, it should be noted that many in the finance profession believe that commissions should be tied to collections and receivables and not paid until the company has collected on the sale. A few companies do take this approach, but it is something that most sales professionals will resist. However, taking this stance puts an end to:

- Sales to entities of questionable credit quality
- Sales with extended payment terms as an inducement
- Other games salespeople sometimes play to increase their commissions at the expense of their employer

The benefit of this is that it doesn't open the door for an unscrupulous employee looking for ways to "enhance" his or her income.

There are a number of things savvy managers can do to prevent this type of thing happening at their organization. For starters, make sure there is an appropriate review or approval process of figures turned in to payroll. Other tactics that will help keep these games in check include:

- A periodic review of commissions against the financials to ensure that they are not rising as sales are falling.
- A policy and procedure review to ensure that you recover commissions when sales are canceled or goods are returned.
- An annual review of your commission policy to ensure that it is in line with the industry and accurately reflects any changes in your business structure.
- Take a close look at the commissions paid your best performers. Have they truly earned them, or have they found a weakness in your commission structure and are exploiting it? This goes hand in hand with your annual review of your commission policy.

FALSE WORKERS' COMPENSATION CLAIMS

We've all heard of the dishonest employees who fake injuries in order to collect disability payments. While we'd like to think that these individuals reside mainly on TV in detective shows, unfortunately, that is not the case. In fact, there have been a number of instances where employees have held other full-time jobs while their employers paid them to stay home and recuperate from some imagined illness. Occasionally, they have had help in this arena from crooked physicians who take kickbacks from the employees receiving the benefits.

Organizations can be harmed financially in two ways when an employee collects a workers' compensation claim fraudulently. If the organization self-insures, as a number of larger organizations do, the money comes right off their bottom line. If, however, they use an insurance company, they will ultimately see their insurance premiums for this coverage rise. This is *not* a victimless crime.

The steps that you can take to protect your organization from this type of fraud are not pretty. Obviously, you want to make the work environment as safe as possible. Some professions suggest that organizations have cameras in the workplace to capture accidents on tape. That way, there is a record. While no one wants to deny a legitimate claim, it is not fair to the rest of your employees if one person takes advantage.

Clearly, your company policy should be that all accidents be reported immediately. That makes it possible to insist on immediate medical attention as well as take other necessary steps. If the claim is large enough, some organizations require a second opinion regarding the extent of the injury.

And, finally, in cases where fraud is suspected, you can hire a private investigator to monitor employees who are on paid disability leave. As we indicated at the beginning of this section, the tactics are not pretty but, unfortunately, given the level of this kind of fraud, may be necessary.

SOME OVERALL PREVENTION TACTICS

As you might have been able to tell as you read through the various sections above, some of the tactics you employ will prevent more than one type of payroll fraud. In this section we'll review a few of the strategies that will help across the board with several types of fraud.

It can't be repeated too often: segregation of duties is critical. Don't let the same employee handle all cash functions. This can be prevalent at smaller companies. The following chores should not be handled by the same person:

- Bookkeeping
- Collections
- Check writing
- Bank account reconciliation

It is generally a good idea to have one employee review payroll data entered into your system by another employee. This is not a 100 percent guarantee of no fraud, but it will require collusion on the part of both employees. Anytime collusion is required for a fraud to occur, your risk drops dramatically.

A timely and regular review of the bank statements will also help. This is a task that no one really likes to do, but the review is crucial.

Finally, don't overlook your budget process. Investigate all situations where actual payroll costs are higher than budgeted. This is a red flag that needs to be explained. Perhaps there was excessive overtime required on a project, but if that is the case, it can be explained. Budget variances can be the first sign of trouble.

FRAUD IN THE REAL WORLD

Here are some stories from readers and the newspapers illustrating the points made above. To my mind, some of them prove that life is indeed stranger than fiction.

- The payroll clerk prepared all aspects of the payroll, calculating hours worked and taxes withheld, generating checks and preparing payroll tax deposits and reports. The only duty he was not responsible for was signing of the checks, which the owner did. Realizing that the owner was concerned only with the net check issued and never required a report indicating gross wages, he grossed up his check by several thousand dollars per pay period. He also adjusted his federal withholding and Social Security deductions upward to generate the net check he had always received. He filed his tax returns and received extremely large refunds. Despite his having stolen over $100,000, he was not prosecuted. However, he was fired.

- The employee responsible for timekeeping within the department submitted accurate reports for the manager to sign each week. Then she would go into the system and reclassify the hours. Thus, a vacation day might be changed to a sick day or a travel day. She adjusted not only her own time but also that of her friends. At year end, when reviewing the vacation time outstanding report, the manager became suspicious. How could she have so much vacation time remaining when she was out so much? He had IT run a report showing all the changes made to the employee records, and it quickly became apparent what was going on. When confronted with the evidence, the employee admitted what she had done. The company let her go.

CONCLUDING THOUGHTS

Many executives find it hard to believe that their employees would steal from them. They find it especially difficult when it comes to payroll fraud. However, numbers don't lie. According to the Association of Certified Fraud Examiners' 2006 *Report to the Nation*, 13.2 percent of all asset misappropriation fraud was payroll fraud. And the dollar amount involved, while not huge, was not insignificant either. The average fraud was for $50,000. This is nothing to sneeze at. As part of your comprehensive fraud prevention and detection procedures, don't forget to include the safeguards necessary to guard against payroll fraud. Regrettably, it could happen to you.

12

TELECOM FRAUD: YES, IT CAN HAPPEN TO YOU

Why is telecom fraud so frightening, and why are we including it in this book? Because, according to Mark Evans, principal of BottaBoom Consulting LLC, a national telecommunication expense management firm, phone fraud has the potential to put your organization out of business, and that is a truly scary proposition. Despite huge advances in security technology and increased telecommunication security protection and customer awareness, phone fraud continues to be a major concern for all organizations, says Evans, who provided all the information for this chapter.

He warns that even with the advent of voice over Internet protocol (VOIP) technology, thieves have continued to figure out how to hack even the most complicated systems, so organizations of all sorts can still suffer as a result. Just the thought of the possibility of thousands of dollars in losses to a business because of phone fraud is daunting. That is why we have included this valuable information in this book.

TYPES OF PHONE FRAUD

There are four primary kinds of phone fraud that readers should be concerned with:

1. Nuisance fraud (cramming and slamming)
2. Proprietary phone system (private branch exchange [PBX] and key system) fraud

3. Voice mail fraud
4. VOIP phone system fraud—the latest entry into the catalog of frauds

NUISANCE FRAUD

Most organizations will at some time or another encounter nuisance fraud, otherwise known as slamming and cramming. Nuisance fraud usually cannot make or break a business when it strikes, but it can drain revenues if left unchecked on the phone bill.

Cramming occurs when a third-party provider charges for services or fees that the customer has not authorized. These charges are neither ordered nor desired by your company. These charges can include products and services such as bogus voice mail service charges, operator-assisted calls, calling card programs, monthly service fees, and credit check services. These charges are often assessed by dishonest third-party suppliers of data and communication service that phone companies are required, by law, to allow the third-party to place on the bill.

Also, bogus yellow pages and white pages advertising can also mysteriously appear on your business phone bills or be billed to you directly.

EXAMPLES OF CRAMMING

Have you ever looked at your local telephone bill and seen odd charges from "other service providers?" If you have, chances are very good that you've been crammed. For large businesses, the charges are buried deeply in the bills and are difficult to notice, and can go on for years, month after month without being noticed. Below is an example of how one customer's actual cramming charges appear on their phone bill, which contains thousands of pages and thousands of charges:

4159195667 10/25 809 10-04 QBA SERVICES,   INC-VOQBA SERVICES, INC- $12.95
VOICEMAL $12.95

The scrutiny of thousands of pages of phone bills to find this one entry was not easy, let alone the labor involved to investigate and correct the charges. At first glance, the charge of $12.95 for the month looks legitimate for voice mail services. However, it is not. This example came from BottaBoom's practice. When they inquired with the local telephone company (AT&T), they were told the charges are billed on behalf of QBA Services, Inc. through ILD Teleservices (an often used billing clearinghouse for crammers). When the BottaBoom rep called ILD Teleservices, he was provided with the contact number for QBA Services. The charges were disputed in full, and a refund was issued for the all of the previous six months that incurred charges.

U.S. phone regulations make this kind of activity perfectly legal for the crammers. Some companies have hundreds of these kinds of fraudulent charges on their invoices. Few have the resources, patience, or knowledge to address them correctly.

GETTING REFUNDS AND COMBATING CRAMMING

How can you get refunds and combat cramming? First, call your local phone provider and ask them to reverse the charges to the offending party. In most cases, they will. Next, as was done in the previous example, have your local phone company provide you with the number of the dishonest third-party billing clearinghouse entity and number of the company who charges the costs through them.

The clearinghouse entity is merely a billing outlet for the offenders through which they can legally invoice the bogus charges. The clearinghouse cannot refund your bill; you must get to the company that authorizes the clearinghouse entity to bill you. The clearinghouse entity must and usually will supply you with the phone number of the offending company.

Once you get the offending company's number from the billing entity, call the company and tell the representative that you are the only one authorized to approve third-party charges and that you did not authorize the charges, and be sure to cancel the service and ask for full back refunds. Be aware that they'll do everything in their power to convince you that one of your employees made the calls or someone at your company did in fact authorize the charges.

They'll likely even have the name of someone at your company, who they'll allege approved the transaction. They might even claim that they have a recording of a person from your company actually authorizing the cost. Don't buy it! Insist on hearing the recording. Even if they supply a name, that does not mean the charge was in any way authorized. In most cases, they won't be able to produce any factual verification for the charge and they'll back down.

If they persist on billing you, tell them that you intend to file a complaint with the Federal Communications Commission and the Federal Trade Commission. Thereafter, ask your local phone service provider to place a block on all third-party billing, and while you're at it, restrict all 900, 976, and collect calls.

SLAMMING

Slamming can occur when there is an unauthorized switch or change of a carrier providing local, local toll, or long distance service. Slamming is frustrating because dishonest phone companies are able easily to change or "pic" your long distance service to their plans, often at a much higher rate than your preferred or selected carrier had provided. Even after you discover the fraud, there is still the headache of switching all of your lines back to the long distance provider you should have and getting the fraudulent service to issue you a refund.

How do you prevent it? Ask the carrier to put a "pic freeze" on your phone lines. Insist on a corporate password for access on your all of your local, cellular, and long distance phone accounts and restrict all access to those accounts to two key people in your company.

PHONE SYSTEM AND VOICE MAIL FRAUD

Phone system and voice mail frauds continue to be problematic for many companies and will continue to persist as long as companies have PBX and key-type phone systems in place, long distance calls cost money, and hackers can easily gain access. Proactive prevention of this type of fraud is much easier than correcting it once it's occurred. Let's face it, as we've pointed out elsewhere in this book, most criminals are lazy and hackers are no different. They'll leave your company alone and go someplace else if your system has the necessary safeguards in place.

First, make sure that your phone system manufacturer-provided master default passwords for your phone and voice mail systems are changed at your location. Hackers know these passwords and can easily hack your system if they can get access. In fact, many of these phone system master passwords (i.e., Avaya, Siemens, Nortel, Mitel, Cisco) are posted on the Internet, available to anyone. A password change can be done by placing a call to the company that maintains your phone systems.

Also, make sure that your remote access to your phone systems is secure. This can often be done by using security encryption *# 38* technology for remote access to your system.

Next, make sure that your employees do not use easy passwords like "1111" or "0000" to access their voice mail boxes. These can be easily hacked. Also, set your voice mail system to automatically prompt and ensure that employees to change their passwords every 90 days at minimum.

When employees leave the company, make sure that you delete their unused voice mail boxes as quickly as possible. Why? You are not going to believe this one until you read it. The hacker takes control of the voice mail box and records the word *yes*. He then places a third-party call and instructs the outside operator to call the number of your departed employee's old mail box. The operator says, "Do you accept third-party charges for Mr. Jones's call?," and the voice mail box answers, "Yes," as programmed.

SOCIAL ENGINEERING FRAUD

Another major threat to companies today is the problem of weak links in personnel, particularly the company receptionist. This is sometimes referred to as *social engineering fraud*. Employees and your receptionist should be alert for a call that is received whereby an individual may identify him/herself as someone working for the phone company who is testing lines. They might say, "I'm with the phone company and I'm running a test on your phone systems. Please transfer me to extension 90 or 900."

Transferring a caller to those digits first accesses an outside phone line dialing "9," and dialing the "0" accesses the outside operator, who can facilitate a call to anywhere in the world for the crooks. The calls are then back billed to your company.

Hackers have also been known to use other ploys like finding out who the board members are for large companies and then impersonating those individuals on a call to that company. The receptionist may not be able to recognize their voice because typically board members don't interact with receptionists as much as employees do. However, due to a board member's prestige, power, or reputation in the company, the receptionists are well aware of their power, so the caller is able to get unlimited transferring ability to commit his crimes. The crime usually is not discovered until after the arrival of the phone bill. Warn the receptionist and employees of this ploy. Numerous companies are milked for thousands of dollars in overseas calls because of this crime.

If your business has a toll-free inbound number, be on alert! Hackers can call in on the toll-free number and use codes and features to place calls overseas or ring up service charges on paid calling services. What numbers are these hackers dialing and how can you prevent them from out-dialing certain countries and areas from your company phone system? Have your PBX maintenance service provider block calling to the following options on your in-house phone system:

Restrict:
- 0 or 00 dialing
- 0700
- 101xxx0, 101xxxx00, 101xxxx011 (dial-around services)
- 1-900
- 1xxx976
- 976
- 540

Block access to the following high toll fraud countries:
- Bahamas (1–242)
- Commonwealth of the Northern Mariana Islands (1–670)
- St. Vincent and the Grenadines (1–784)
- Trinidad and Tobago (1–868)
- Ivory Coast (country code 225)
- Mali (country code 223)
- Pakistan (country code 92)
- Senegal (country code 221)
- Yemen (country code 967)
- Caribbean (country code 809)

CALL FORWARDING/CONFERENCING PROBLEMS

Restrict some call forwarding and conferencing features on your company phone system that might assist hackers in forwarding calls on your dime. Also, you can restrict collect calling and third-party calling, and third-party billing (with some carriers).

Arrange to meet with your phone system vendor to conduct a vulnerability analysis to ensure that your phone system is secure. Most of the larger telephone equipment manufacturing vendors—Siemens, Avaya, Nortel, and Mitel—have security bulletins and security support programs to help keep your systems secure and up to date.

VOIP FRAUD

Voice over Internet protocol (VOIP) is the family of technologies that allow IP (Internet protocol) networks to be used for voice applications, such as telephony, voice instant messaging, and tele-conferencing. This last fraud concern to be discussed is the latest threat to companies. While still in its infancy, VOIP fraud is becoming more prevalent. Again, as previously mentioned in the earlier section regarding phone system fraud, one of the best ways to prevent this kind of fraud is to change the system passwords in your VOIP phone system.

There is beginning to be increased attention surrounding recent attacks on VOIP systems, but actual cases of documented fraud are now just starting to become documented. In 2007, two men were arrested because they routed calls through unprotected network ports at other companies to route calls on to providers. Over three weeks, the two routed half a million phone calls to a VOIP provider. Federal investigators believe the two made as much as $1 million from the scam.

Nevertheless, actual cases of VOIP fraud on these systems are still somewhat rare, at least at the present time. However, there is a lot of potential for harm as vulnerabilities and holes in security are becoming more prevalent and more easily exploitable by resource-ful hackers. As with automated clearinghouse (ACH) fraud, we expect it to grow and urge readers to protect themselves.

VOIP hackers can exploit system passwords to gain access to company VOIP voice systems and have and can potentially steal millions of minutes of long distance service. How? Hackers read up on VOIP vendor security bulletins and gather public information on company IP addresses that are posted on the Internet, which allows them to hack into client systems. They devise and use customized software code to decipher access codes and access exposed data ports and data gateways and computer systems. Hackers can find it easy to use default or poorly chosen passwords.

To counteract these attacks on your company and keep updated with the latest security technology and VOIP fraud prevention advice, consult with your VOIP equipment vendors and ask specific questions on how to best protect your systems. If you have a large VOIP system, it may make sense for you to have a professional conduct a security audit on your system. IP business consumers and IT managers need to use the latest encryption techniques for their network access and train and monitor their employees on effective safeguarding of their company data and IP system information.

FRAUD IN THE REAL WORLD

Here are some stories from readers and the newspapers illustrating the points made above. To my mind, some of them prove that life is indeed stranger than fiction.

- A "trusted and respected veteran" telephone repair technician was making unauthorized overseas long distance calls (an inside job) to the tune of about $50 to $60 per week, calling his brother who was serving in the U.S. military in South Korea. It was picked up because, on the call accounting reports, it was noticed that the calls were going out at 5 A.M., before regular business hours from a closed bank branch. A company employee working on the audit happened to find that number written in the technician's handwriting on a slip of paper located at his workstation in the phone room. When confronted, the trusted technician turned beet red and quickly confessed. Sure enough, security access system records and logs confirmed that he was on site at the corporate headquarters at those times. He did not need to be located physically at the remote bank branch to commit his crimes. He simply configured a remote phone at the bank branch in software on the main phone system and dialed away at 5 A.M. He was terminated immediately from his job of 22 years, and he paid back our client in full.

- A Fortune 500 company's phone bills ballooned by tens of thousands of dollars during the months of November and December. At first, we thought it was just their busy season for orders; however, after more digging, it was discovered that hundreds of employees regularly called their loved ones in other states to say hello over the holidays. They did not know that this type of action was prohibited. It had always seemed to be just part of the corporate culture—an acceptable thing to do. The employer put in a written policy that restricted all long distance calls, unless specifically approved by a manager, and managers were now required to sign call reports delivered to them each month. The phone bill expenses during the holidays (and at other times) dropped like a rock.

CONCLUDING THOUGHTS

Clearly, someone with a little knowledge can do a lot of harm to your organization via this type of fraud. The information provided by Evans is enough for any organization to get some basic protections in place. Telecom audit firms are another way to help uncover fraud. Groups such as Evans's BottaBoom Consulting LLC (www.bottaboom.com) will audit your telecom bills looking for charges that do not belong. Since they work on a contingency basis, they cost nothing if they find nothing. At the same time, they are best situated with their specialized knowledge to find frauds that would otherwise go unnoticed. This is an issue no organization can afford to ignore—there's just too much money at risk.

PART TWO

Strategies to Deter, Prevent, and Detect All Sorts of Accounts Payable Fraud

By now, your head may be spinning as you look at all the places where a fraudster could attack your organization and walk away with its money. You may even be wondering how to plug so many "opportunities" for fraud. The answer is simple; many—although definitely not all—of the controls are the same. What you do in one arena will help in others.

Similarly, there are certain really bad practices that many organizations still use without realizing how easy these practices make life for the crooks looking to defraud you. By eliminating those practices, discussed in this Part, you will also take a dent out of your "fraud potential."

The goal of this book is to provide you with strategies that will ideally deter fraud completely so no one, either your employees or outsiders, even considers trying to defraud you. In all likelihood, that goal will not be 100 percent achievable, and the next step would be to prevent fraud, should someone be foolish enough to try it on your watch. And, finally, if everything else fails—and it will occasionally—the strategies you put in place will help you detect any fraud that has occurred.

The reality is that you can never stop fraud 100 percent. But you can make it so difficult that the crooks decide your organization is just not worth the effort and take their business elsewhere. The strategies discussed in this section should put you on the right fraud prevention and detection path.

13

BEST PRACTICES—NOT: TACTICS THAT UNINTENTIONALLY PROMOTE FRAUD

If I were to simplify this chapter into a few lines, it would be this: Poor accounts payable practices unintentionally promote fraud, while strong ones prevent it and duplicate payments. Your employees know where all the weaknesses in your processes are. So if you employ any of the practices discussed in the rest of this chapter, you are opening the door should one of your employees decide he or she would like to supplement his or her income at your expense. Let's take a look at ten really bad accounts payable practices that facilitate fraud:

1. *Allowing employees to share passwords and user IDs.* This happens all the time, and then when fraud occurs, it is impossible to figure out who did it, although you can be certain of one thing: It wasn't the person whose password was used. Have a clear company policy, shared with every employee, about how seriously you take this issue. Make it clear that if passwords are shared, the employees involved will be fired.

2. *Employees who write their passwords and user IDs on a piece of paper or Post-It and then tape it to their computer for easy reference*—both theirs and, unfortunately, the crook looking to pass along the blame for the theft he or she committed.

3. *Returning checks to anyone other than the payee.* Checks should be mailed—period, end of story. There should be #40

145

few, if any, exceptions, and those exceptions should require written authorization from a high-level executive, along with a written request explaining why the check needs to be returned. And that explanation better have a good business reason, not the usual reason: Joe in purchasing is going out to lunch and wants to give the vendor the check.

4. *Not issuing a purchase order (PO) at the moment the order is placed.* In the very worst-case scenario (and this is a true story), one satellite location of a bigger company would wait until the invoice was received and then use the invoice to create the PO. I don't know if the vendors realized this, for if they did, I wonder about the pricing on the invoices and the accuracy of the amounts ordered. With this approach, there would be no way to track down duplicate payments, inaccurate pricing, overcharging for shipping, or fraud. It should be a company policy that the PO be filled out completely at the time the order is placed—not afterwards.

5. *Making every employee over a certain level an authorized check signer.* This was a common practice 20 years ago. It just asks for trouble when an employee is discharged, especially if the bank isn't notified in a timely manner. While this may be a nice way to raise morale and treat employees well, it causes too many problems to be considered a reasonable practice. The reality is, especially with employees having nothing to do with the payment process, when these employees leave the company, no one thinks about notifying the bank to remove them as signers.

6. *Not doing reference checks of employees hired in accounts payable or to deal with your money.* While reference checks are not perfect, they do provide a certain level of comfort and, should anything go wrong, demonstrate some due diligence on your part.

7. *Not appropriately storing check stock.* In the worst case of this, an organization bought checks from a company in

another city. This in and of itself was fine. However, the check-printing company mailed the checks in a box stamped "Checks Enclosed." So, what do you think happened while the checks were in transit? Assuming your check printer is smart enough not to label your checks in such a manner, it is still important to keep your check stock stored away so no one who isn't supposed to have it can get their hands on it.

8. *Not using positive pay.*
9. *Having a petty cash box.* This is just an invitation to petty thievery.
10. *Not having an explicit, written travel and entertainment (T&E) policy shared with every affected party.* Today, it can be posted on your Internet or intranet site, eliminating the "I didn't know that" or "No one ever told me" excuse.
11. *Not having appropriate segregation of duties.*
12. *Not having strong internal controls.*

CLOSING THOUGHTS

As you look through this list you will note that none of the tactics suggested cost a red cent, although some may require changing the way the organization thinks. It may also require a certain discipline of its employees—a discipline that may be missing. Given the tight margins most organizations run on today, there is no excuse for ignoring these issues. Most organizations simply cannot afford to.

14

FRAUD MONITORING REPORTS: A NECESSARY EVIL

Few people want to admit that their organization might be a victim of fraud. Yet, as you are by now painfully aware, it happens and it happens across the board to virtually every type of organization. No one is exempt. Strong internal controls and appropriate segregation of duties will go a long way to limiting the damage. However, they can't completely stop it. Some employees are quite adept at finding the weaknesses in your systems and procedures and exploiting them. Savvy managers recognize the need to periodically review their records to detect frauds that might have snuck through.

AUTOMATED MONITORING

There are sophisticated and expensive software packages you can buy for the purpose of monitoring, sometimes on a continual basis. One such product is APEX Analytix FirstStrike™ Fraud Detect software, a comprehensive software solution that provides the continuous monitoring companies need to fight fraud in the accounts payable disbursement process.

While these packages are wonderful, for many they are overkill. Quite a few organizations choose not to use them, but rather develop a series of reports using Excel or Access.

These reports can be run and reviewed by internal audit or, if there is no internal audit function, by someone in accounting. It goes without saying that the person running and reviewing these reports should have nothing to do with the payment function or any of the files used in the reports.

The frequency of these reports is something the management team of each organization will have to determine. In all likelihood, there will be reports that are run on an annual basis, some that are run monthly, and others that are run on an as-needed basis. The last group is run only when suspicious activity raises questions.

HOW ANYONE CAN RUN REPORTS

The information discussed in the remainder of the chapter relates to the various recommended reports. The information in each section will be extracted from the appropriate files and dumped into Excel or Access, depending on which is appropriate and which the end user has more comfort with.

Once the information is in the program, it can be manipulated to accommodate the requirements of the organization. It should be noted that some organizations use Crystal Reports and others use pivot tables in concert with their fraud monitoring. If you have any other tools that you regularly use and are comfortable with, feel free to dump the information into that program and manipulate it accordingly.

The important issue here is not which tool is used to analyze the data but rather that the data is extracted and analyzed on a very regular basis. For the purposes of this chapter, we are going to talk about the simplest tool, Excel. However, realize that you can dump the data into whatever tool you are most comfortable using.

A WORD ABOUT MORE SOPHISTICATED MONITORING

It should be noted that there are many more advanced and intricate reports that analysts and statisticians can run to look for fraud possibilities. They are well beyond the scope of this book and generally require mathematical and analytical skills that only a few of our readers will have. Some of the approaches used by those with these advanced skills include:

- Regression analysis
- Monte Carlo simulations
- Benford's law
- Ratio analysis
- Trend analysis

HOW MUCH CHECKING IS ENOUGH?

The answer to this question varies from organization to organization. Clearly, the larger the organization, the more it might want to check. There are other factors that affect this decision. Some of them include: # 42

- How strong are the internal controls?
- Are there segregation-of-duties concerns?
- Have there been fraud attempts on the organization recently?
- Is management suspicious?
- Have there been any anonymous tips?
- Have others in your industry been hit with fraud?
- Have others in your geographic location been hit with fraud?
- Is employee discontent high?
- Have there been layoffs or staff cutbacks?
- Were annual increases unusually low?
- Have any unpopular policies been introduced recently?

Don't stick your head in the sand when answering these questions. Too often, an unpopular initiative is announced, and management, wanting to believe the staff understands how it will be better for the organization as a whole, sticks its head in the sand when evaluating its impact. If the answer to any of these questions is affirmative, fraud monitoring should be stepped up.

Remember, a discontented employee will use that disgruntlement to rationalize defrauding the organization. And your employees know where the weaknesses in your processes are.

THE BIG REPORT EVERYONE SHOULD RUN

If you run only one report, this is the one. We've mentioned it several times throughout this book. The employee data from human resources should be run against the master vendor file. This is to identify instances where an employee may be defrauding the company and using his or her own information to do it. Many of these thefts will involve an employee using either his or her own home address or Social Security number. Why? Because they are either too lazy to set up a completely phony entity for the fraud or it never occurs to them that anyone will check.

The reason is irrelevant. Take the data you get from human resources and dump it into the Excel spreadsheet. Then take the information from your master vendor file. Here are two simple checks you can do with that information:

1. *Look for duplicate addresses.* While occasionally there may be a legitimate duplicate, most of the time after employees' T&E activity is removed, the duplicate signals trouble.
2. *Look for duplicate taxpayer identification numbers (TINs).* Again, there are very few legitimate instances where you should find a duplicate, especially if T&E activity has been removed. If you are using the IRS's TIN-matching program (which I strongly recommend), you will have only legitimate TINs in your files.

This report should be run once a year, and it should be run every year. If you are lucky, you will never find a match.

THE EASY REPORT

While you have all the data dumped into the Excel spreadsheet, check your human resources data for duplicate addresses. Again, there are very few legitimate reasons why two paychecks should be associated with the same address, unless you have two or more people from the same family or roommates working for the same company.

Since you have the data from human resources, also ask for the direct deposit account numbers. Look for duplicates. Unless you have married employees sharing a bank account, two paychecks are unlikely to have a good reason for being deposited into the same bank account.

Again, while you have the data dumped into the file, look for #43 the same TIN associated with more than one employee. This can signal phantom employees.

Run this data at least once a year.

Obviously, when either of these reports is run, care should be taken, as there is confidential employee data involved. Access to the data and the reports should be limited.

OTHER FRAUD DETECTION REPORTS

Inventory

While you have your employees' addresses, compare them to the "ship to" addresses in the master vendor file. You may discover one of your employees having goods shipped to his or her home.

Payment Data

One of the problems across the board is payments right under the level where a manager's approval is needed. It is an ongoing issue with travel and entertainment (T&E) reimbursements where receipts are not required for expenditures over a certain dollar level, say $25. Requiring receipts for everything over $5 usually ends that problem.

A number of years ago I worked for an organization where the chief operating officer (COO) signed every check. He was quite strict and questioned anything he thought inappropriate. This was a colossal waste of his time, but it enabled him to see everything, including everyone's T&E. After much analysis and the implementation of strong internal controls, he was convinced to let all checks under $1,000 go out with only one signature on them. When word of this spread, miraculously, there were very few T&E reimbursement requests for over $1,000. Across the board, everyone started putting in more frequent reimbursement requests. Employees would do anything under the sun to keep their reports under the $1,000 limit and away from the COO's scrutiny. Executives who would wait months on end to submit reports were now sending them in every few weeks.

This tale highlights the approval-level issue, not only in T&E, but also for invoice approvals.

Take all your vendor payments and list them in size order. Take a close look at those just below your approval levels. Is there a suspiciously large number of them? Look at those payments even closer. Are there more to one vendor than you would think is reasonable? Your employees know where your approval levels are, and if they are going to try and steal from you using invoice fraud, many will do so right under the dollar amount where an approval or second approval is required.

You may discover something else going on. Knowing what your approval levels are, it is possible that your employees instructed a vendor to send several invoices rather than one, in order to avoid having to get the necessary approvals. So, what you may uncover is not necessarily fraud, but an employee effectively purchasing outside his or her approval levels. While this is not as bad as fraud, it is something that should be corrected.

While you have that list of payments in front of you, look for even amounts. Rather than submit a phony invoice for $23,497, crooks will often bill for $25,000. Take a closer look at even-amount transactions. There is a higher chance they are not legit, although clearly many of them will be. Yes, I know; if the crooks had half a brain in their head, they would bill for an odd amount, but more than a few don't.

Rush Check Data

As discussed in Chapter 2, a higher percentage of rush checks turn out to be for fraudulent purposes. So, in addition to being extremely inefficient for the accounts payable operations, there is another good reason to avoid them. If you have been successful in getting the number down to a few a month, this report will need to be run only once a year. However, if rush checks are a continuing problem, the report should be run more frequently. Here's what you should do.

Download the rush check data along with vendor IDs and the name of the processor who handled them. If possible, also get the name of the person who approved the invoice in question for payment. Then summarize the data by:

- Vendor
- Processor
- Approver

 # 44

If there are more than one or two checks in any category, you need to start an investigation immediately. If all rush checks are assigned to one processor, that category will not be relevant to this process. What this should uncover is either a process that needs to be fixed or fraud.

Remember the story in Chapter 8—the consultant who claimed it was easier to get a rooster to lay an egg on a picket fence in New York City in July than to get paid on time? His name would have stood out like a sore thumb if such an analysis had been completed.

Master Vendor File

Savvy employees with larceny in their hearts know that the master vendor file can provide the cover they need to hide their frauds against their employer if the appropriate controls are not in place. And the truth is that controls in the master vendor file of many organizations are lacking. So if you have not cleansed your master vendor file either in the past few years or ever, know two things:

1.   You need to do it right away, as inactive vendors can provide refuge for an employee looking to hide transactions.
2.   You have a lot of company.

But this is one of those times when the fact that "everybody does it" is not an acceptable excuse.

The first master vendor file report should list every vendor without a TIN and/or phone number in your file. If your policies for setting up new vendors are sloppy, you will have many legitimate vendors on this list. However, if you require, as you should, some basic information before a vendor is set up, any vendors on this list should be suspect. The combined policy of requiring a TIN and running the TINs through the IRS's TIN-matching program will make it virtually impossible for someone to set up a phony vendor in your master vendor file. Of course, they will still be able to set up legitimate vendors who do not belong in your files.

Be very careful of dormant accounts in your master vendor file. Thieving employees submitting fraudulent invoices use these accounts to get their invoices processed. If you do not have sufficient controls on the master vendor file, they simply put in a change of address, and then have the fraudulent check come to their home or wherever they have decided to have the checks delivered.

That is why it is so important to have a report run every week or every month (whichever is appropriate for your organization), showing all changes to the master vendor file. This report should be delivered to a very senior executive, who should review it. This fact should not be a secret. If this fact is public enough, it may be enough to prevent games with the addresses in the master vendor file.

In reality, few high-level executives have the time to review such a report. They can delegate it to a meticulous subordinate who has the authority to request the backup for any entry to the file. These requests should come under the senior executive's name. Even if there is nothing amiss, several requests for backup should be made periodically. If you do this well, you may never have fraud related to games with the master vendor file. So, please, do not take the fact that you never discover any wrongdoing as a signal to stop the report. Just the opposite; take the lack of fraud due to master vendor file manipulations as a signal that your actions are preventing it.

Periodically, request a report showing sudden activity in inactive accounts. The length of inactivity will depend on the nature of your business. Some suggest this report should be run monthly, showing activity on accounts that have had no activity in the past six months. You will need to keep in mind when analyzing this report that you may have seasonal vendors from whom you purchase only once or twice a year.

Vendors' Invoice Numbers

Download, by vendor, your suppliers' invoice numbers. Then review the invoice numbers by vendor. Vendors submitting fraudulent invoices will often do so with no gaps between their invoice numbers. This trick is similar to the employee who buys a receipt pad commonly used by waitresses and then submits them in order. A smart thief will submit invoices with invoice numbers out of order so it will appear your invoice is part of a normal progression. Often, however, especially in the case of an employee, they get lazy and do not do this.

Once you get the report, review it to see if the invoices are fraudulent or the vendor simply doesn't invoice many customers. Your knowledge of your supplier community should provide the answer to this issue.

Duplicate Payments

One of the beauties of installing controls to stop or limit duplicate payments is that they generally also work to thwart fraud. Thus, it is a good idea to have a duplicate payment audit done by an outside firm at least once every two years. Since most charge on a contingency basis, if you are employing best practices, your cost should be low—and your bottom line will still come out ahead of the game as you recover funds paid in error. Good duplicate payment audit firms will also point out where your weaknesses are. They will give you a list of recommendations on what you can do to minimize duplicate payments in the future. At the same time, by implementing their suggestions, you will make it harder for the fraudsters trying to illicitly get their hands on your organization's money.

Before talking a little about the reports to identify duplicate payments, let me point out that many are not fraud, just an inefficient process. While you will want to recover the duplicates, they are slightly less troubling than out-and-out fraud.

We recommend that duplicate payment testing be done every time payments are made. For some this will be every day, and for others as infrequently as once or twice a month. Look for duplicate invoice numbers over the past 90 or 180 days; look for duplicate payment amounts (especially if the amount in question is an odd dollar amount). When you find the same invoice number, do a little investigating. It is possible that it appears twice because a partial payment was made. But it may also be a duplicate payment.

Look closely at the invoice numbers. Many systems do not permit the same invoice number to be entered twice for the same vendor. Savvy processors get around this restriction by merely adding a space, period, or extra letter at the end of the invoice number.

Large Adjustments

Journal entries, voids, and manual adjustments are sometimes used by employees to cover fraudulent transactions. Mixing them in with legitimate entries makes it more difficult to detect those entries that are designed to cover the fraud.

Run a report showing the number of adjustments, voids, and journal entries by employee. Investigate any that seem to be disproportionately high for the employee's work or in comparison to peers doing similar work. To accurately analyze this data you will need someone who is familiar with the work. Needless to say, if any of these adjustments are against inactive accounts, further investigation should be conducted immediately.

Off-Hour Activity

One of the things fraud examiners have discovered is that thieves tend to commit their fraud after working hours. If you can get a listing from your information technology (IT) group of employees who access the systems and make adjustments outside normal work hours, get it and examine it in conjunction with your other reports.

Obviously, some hardworking employees will legitimately access the system after most of your employees have gone home. However, a disproportionate number of thefts, especially if they involve adjustments to your financial reporting system, do occur after hours.

THE ACT LIST

Over time, your staff will develop an A list, or Always Check Thoroughly (ACT) list. These are the vendors and employees (in *#45* the case of T&E reimbursements) who routinely have errors on their invoices. Every organization has them. Inevitably, these errors will be in their favor at the expense of your bottom line. Your accounts payable manager can probably rattle off the names on his or her list without referencing the computer.

Whether these employees and vendors intend to defraud the organization or are just sloppy is irrelevant. Make sure any invoices or reimbursement requests from these parties are checked thoroughly, no matter how small the dollar amount involved. When errors are found, make the other party aware and pay only the correct amount, even if the error is small. Let them know by your actions that you are watching and have no intention of letting an extra nickel slip through. Eventually, most of them will realize they are wasting their time and stop. But never take them off your ACT list or they'll start up again.

CLOSING THOUGHTS

Clearly, there are many reports you can run to detect and prevent fraud on your watch. The key is to keep it in proportion to your risk—not getting carried away but not ignoring the risk either. If you've never run any fraud detection reports, it might be a good idea to run a number of the ones discussed in this chapter. A discussion with either your internal audit staff or your external auditor will guide you after that. They may have additional reports you can run as well. After reviewing the results, come up with a few that will do the trick for you. Then run them regularly, even if you have no fraud. This is one area where you cannot afford to let your guard down.

Here's one last thought to consider when evaluating your various fraud risk assessments. While we generally recommend spot checking when it comes to T&E expense reporting, many organizations do not take that best practice approach. The reason is that many larger frauds have come to light because the employee couldn't resist the allure of cheating on his or her T&E expense report. When that fraud was uncovered and the investigation began, larger frauds came to light—because the fact is that most thieves are nothing if not greedy.

15

FRAUD DETECTION AND PREVENTION: SIMPLE TACTICS YOU CAN USE

Before we take a look at what you can do to prevent and detect fraud, it is important to understand just exactly how fraud is detected. This provides some clues to what you have to do to prevent it. There are two studies that addressed this issue. While their numbers aren't exactly the same, they tell a very similar, albeit disconcerting, story.

2006 *REPORT TO THE NATION* FRAUD DETECTION

In its very popular survey, the Association of Fraud Examiners (ACFE) discovered that fraud was uncovered in the following ways:

Tip	34.2%
By accident	25.4
Internal audit	20.2
Internal controls	19.2
External audit	12.0
Notified by police	3.8

In some cases two methods were credited for the discovery. Hence, the figures add up to more than 100 percent. What becomes crystal clear right off the bat is that detection is often beyond anything the organization might do. Given all the efforts in this regard, it is kind of disconcerting.

PRICEWATERHOUSECOOPERS 2007 GLOBAL ECONOMIC CRIME SURVEY FRAUD DETECTION

The PricewaterhouseCoopers report tells a similar tale. Its survey shows that fraud was detected in the following ways:

Tip (internal)	21%
Internal audit	19
Other	15
Tip (external)	14
Whistleblower	8
By accident	6
Fraud risk management	4
Suspicious transaction reporting	4
Corporate security	4
Law enforcement	3
Rotation of personnel	3

Once again, over half the discoveries had nothing to do with what the organization did but were pure luck.

The numbers from these surveys scream for the need for anonymous hotlines.

ANONYMOUS HOTLINES

In fact, the Sarbanes-Oxley Act requires listed U.S. companies, as well as non-U.S. companies listed on a U.S. stock exchange, to establish procedures for dealing with confidential, anonymous employee submissions regarding questionable accounting or auditing matters. Whether required by law or not, the establishment of such a hotline is a really good idea, as demonstrated by the numbers above.

The first complaint that some managers have with anonymous hotlines is the concern about disgruntled employees making fraudulent complaints on the hotline—and the odds are good that will happen. But upon investigation those complaints can be weeded out. When the minor inconvenience of dealing with those disgruntled employees is weighed against the financial gain that can be had, it should be a no-brainer. And for a public company, it is required by law.

WHAT COMPANIES CAN DO TO PREVENT FRAUD

While good internal controls and appropriate segregation of duties are the first steps to preventing fraud, there are other things that organizations can do to minimize occupational fraud. Some of the tactics recommended by the ACFE include:

- Fraud hotlines
- Anonymous reporting mechanisms
- Ethics training
- Internal audit
- Surprise audits
- External auditors

While these will not necessarily prevent all frauds, they help uncover these cases when they do occur. The ACFE found that:

- 75 percent had external auditors.
- 59 percent had internal auditors.
- Under half had fraud training and fraud hotlines.
- Only 29 percent had surprise audits.

The study also noted that fraud hotlines and internal audits, as well as fraud awareness and ethics training, appear to significantly reduce the size and length of frauds.

SIMPLE TACTICS TO MAKE SURE NO ONE ROBS THE TILL ON YOUR WATCH

No one likes to think that it could happen at their company, but the facts say otherwise. Alas, most of us will experience some sort of fraud in our organization at some point in our careers. Some will be unfortunate enough to have it happen more than once on their watch. What's even worse is that the odds are good that one of your employees will be involved. While it is never possible to completely eliminate fraud, there are some things any organization can do to detect it early before it gets out of hand. Following is a list of eight techniques any organization can use to uncover fraud:

1. *Install an anonymous hotline.* We have to say it again. There are two benefits to this approach—the obvious and the not so obvious. For starters, the hotline provides a mechanism for an employee to report something that doesn't look right without getting involved. Not convinced this is a good idea? The ACFE reports that over one-third of all frauds are uncovered by a tip. Sure, some discontented staff member may use the hotline to cause trouble for another employee, but the odds are high that a good portion of those tips will be legit. There's an even better reason: to lower your losses when a fraud does occur. The ACFE also reports that, "Anonymous fraud hotlines suffered a median loss of $100,000, whereas organizations without hotlines had a median loss of $200,000."

2. *Surprise audits.* The internal audit function should have the authority to go in and audit any group without advance notice. This could be in reaction to an anonymous tip or as part of its regular rotation. This is especially important whenever cash is involved, for example, with a petty cash box.

3. *Run your employees' addresses against the address file of your vendors in the master vendor file.* Any matches should be investigated. There are legitimate reasons why there may be a match but, generally speaking, these are limited. Make sure you make adjustments if your traveling employees are included in the master vendor file.

4. *Create a "Changes to the Master Vendor File" report and have it reviewed by a senior executive.* It should be run periodically as appropriate for your activity, either weekly or

monthly. Its purpose is to identify any unusual or potentially fraudulent activity.

5. *Do a background check on any employee handling money.* Someone who has successfully committed fraud once is likely to repeat it, especially if circumstances put the individual in a situation where personal finances are difficult.

6. *Vendor applications should be required and reviewed in accounts payable or somewhere outside the department recommending the new vendor.* The review can be cursory, simply checking to make sure the vendor exists on public records, and is a control to ensure that an employee isn't setting up a fraudulent vendor.

7. *Employ the "eyeball test" when it comes to reviewing data.* Train your employees to take a step back and look at the data objectively. Does it make sense, or is something out of whack?

8. *When setting up responsibilities, make sure to employ appropriate segregation of duties.* Sometimes when a new function or process is put in place, the segregation issue is completely overlooked.

9. *Don't overlook the three-way match.* For this to work effectively, purchasing must complete purchase orders (POs) with all details and send them to the vendor and accounts payable. Then the receiving dock must be instructed to not just check off the paperwork saying everything was received, but actually count what is in each box and on each pallet and make sure it matches what the receiving documents say. Then, when the invoice arrives in accounts payable, the staff there can match all three and be comfortable knowing three different arms of the organization supplied each piece.

10. *Instruct your employees to use common sense.* Give them the authority to question anything that doesn't look right. Make "because I said so" not acceptable.

11.   *Be suspicious of employees living beyond their means.*   In a big city with its anonymity and two-wage-earner couples, this is not as easy to discern as it might have been 20 or 30 years ago. That assistant driving a BMW might be married to a stock trader. Or he might be dipping into the till. Do a little behind-the-scenes investigating, but do not confront the person unless you have the hard evidence.

12.   *Send a message: prosecute.*   This may sound harsh, and it is. But if fraud is uncovered within your organization and there are serious dollars involved, press charges. This action will make others think twice. If the dollars involved are smaller, firing may be the way to go. This is definitely a case of letting the punishment fit the crime.

FRAUD IN THE REAL WORLD

Here are some stories from readers and the newspapers illustrating the points made above. To my mind, some of them prove that life is indeed stranger than fiction.

- Our organization was the victim of embezzlement, not once but twice, both times by the business manager. Both individuals chose to enrich themselves via the company. They were prosecuted, along with the individuals who conspired with them. Obviously, the firm had some serious internal control issues. These crimes were committed before I started working here, and internal controls have been implemented, though I still see some instances where they could be overridden.

- The fraud took place in our company because management decided not to follow internal controls. We had the same person ordering, receiving, and approving for payment. When he questioned this, the accounts payable manager was told that was his job. Not long after that, the one person who worked with him went to the manager, and they found that they had a problem. The next thing we knew, the employee was taken away in handcuffs.

CLOSING THOUGHTS

If I had to limit what I could do to prevent fraud, and I hope you don't, I would focus on two issues: strengthening internal controls and making sure I had appropriate segregation of duties. The side benefit from these last two tactics is that they also help minimize duplicate payments, so you'd get a double benefit from your actions.

16

SARBANES-OXLEY

A book on fraud in accounts payable would not be complete without mentioning Sarbanes-Oxley. Some of the most egregious frauds in recent times gave rise to the act. While the frauds were far more comprehensive than simple payment deceit, they did impact accounts payable functioning in many organizations. We'll start with a quick overview of the Act and then take a look at its impact on accounts payable.

SARBANES-OXLEY

The Sarbanes-Oxley Act of 2002 is comprised of 66 sections, only a few of which will be referenced. In fact, virtually the entire chapter is devoted to the infamous Section 404, which focuses on internal controls. As virtually everyone reading this is painfully aware, the enactment of this legislation was a direct result of numerous well-publicized accounting scandals, or some would say frauds. The intent was not only to close the loopholes that made these transgressions possible, but also to hold management at the very highest levels responsible for what went on in their companies on their watch.

It was inevitable that increased accountability, in the form of fines and possible jail time, would trickle down to middle management. Few officers would willingly sign financial statements under such dire threats without requiring some sort of a guarantee from the minions who toiled on their behalf. Thus, quickly, subcertifications sprung up. These documents also known as cascading certifications or upstream certifications (depending where you stand) are now found at a significant percentage. However, that requirement rarely affects the accounts payable manager, although it does in a few organizations.

OVERVIEW OF THE ACT

The act is broken into 11 main parts called titles. Each of the titles is further subdivided into portions called sections. The most famous of the sections are probably:

- Whistle-blower protections (i.e., retaliation against informants)
- Auditor independence
- Timely disclosures
- Corporate responsibility for financial reports
- Management assessment of internal controls

While the whistle-blower piece may be the second most interesting section, it does not greatly affect the accounts payable operations. Similarly, while it might be of some interest to talk about chief executive officers and chief financial officers getting fined and possibly going to jail, we are not going to spend a whole lot of time discussing either of these issues.

SARBANES-OXLEY SURVEY

The question plaguing our minds was simple: after all the hoopla that surrounded the Sarbanes-Oxley Act and the implementation of its contents, did it have any effect on accounts payable operations at organizations, both private and public? Now, before you begin to protest that the act applies only to public companies, we'd like to point out that we are aware of this. Yet, we had heard rumblings from organizations that its influence extended beyond public firms. So, we set out to find out.

Accounts Payable Now & Tomorrow recently polled a group of its subscribers on how the Sarbanes-Oxley Act has impacted their operations. To put the issue in perspective, it began by analyzing the corporate structure of the participants. Most were *not* from public companies, making the results all the more interesting. It demonstrates the far-reaching influence the act has had when it comes to the payment practices in the corporate world.

Just under 30 percent of the respondents were from public companies, with the remainder coming from both privately held companies and other institutions such as universities, hospitals, and government entities (such as states, cities, etc.). There were roughly the same number of other institutions in the study as there were public firms, with the remainder being solidly planted in the private sector.

This fact is important as you look at the numbers. It demonstrates the far-reaching impact of the act, not just on public companies, as was first imagined, but also on their peers in the private sector.

IMPACT OF THE ACT ON ACCOUNTS PAYABLE OPERATIONS

Here's how the respondents said the act helped them:

It helped prove that our existing controls were/are effective	28%
Added more controls and/or made changes, which benefit our program	27
It forced the organization to document policies and procedures	19
Processes are now more restrictive due to SOX	9

No one claimed they had to add controls and/or procedures for which the benefit was not apparent, even though they had the option of selecting this. And, alas, no one said that it enabled them to eliminate some really bad practices that they had not been able to eliminate previously. That being said, 29 percent said that the act was the key in obtaining their organization's support to make desired changes. Just under 20 percent (18 percent) of the respondents indicated that the act had no impact on their overall accounts payable operations.

OUTSIDE INFLUENCES

Some organizations have reported that although they are not subject to the strictures of Sarbanes-Oxley, they are complying at the bequest of key customers, their financial institutions, or their suppliers. We wondered if this aspect had trickled down into the accounts payable operations. While most of our respondents, a whopping 70 percent, indicated that this had not happened in their organization, the remainder were evenly split between those who had been asked about their compliance practices and those who were not sure if they had been contacted.

FUNCTIONS IMPROVED

Accounts payable professionals are often advised to use the threat of Sarbanes-Oxley to force changes that should be made. But does this work? Based on what the recipients of the survey said, the answer is a resounding yes.

Exhibit 16.1 shows the areas where the survey respondents were able to make the biggest changes in their operations thanks to the influence of the Sarbanes-Oxley Act. It will come as no surprise to learn that over half the respondents cleaned up their travel and entertainment (T&E) review process. Those involved in accounts payable are well aware of all the problems that can exist in that nebulous function.

T&E reimbursement and review processes	57%
Internal audit reviews	43
Strengthened backup requirements for check requests	43
Records retention policy and processes strengthened	29
1099 reporting	29
Controls on master vendor file	28
Electronic invoicing	28
Invoice approval process	28
Unclaimed property compliance	14
Sales and use tax operations	14
Check issuance process	14
Matching process	14
Invoice handling process	14
Electronic payments	13

EXHIBIT 16.1 PERCENTAGE OF RESPONDENTS WHO ATTRIBUTED THEIR SUCCESS IN IMPROVING VARIOUS FUNCTIONS TO THE SARBANES-OXLEY ACT
Source: Accounts Payable Now & Tomorrow

T&E REIMBURSEMENT AND REVIEW PROCESSES

The biggest across-the-board change has occurred in the T&E processes. Clearly, companies across the board recognize that a lot of the old wink-wink, boys-will-be-boys games that used to go on with employees' T&E expense reports can no longer go on. It appears that almost every organization with loose policies in this arena has cleaned up its act.

A little more than one-quarter of those responding to the survey indicated they had not changed due to the act. In all likelihood, these are the organizations that had their house in order.

INTERNAL AUDIT REVIEWS

Before the passage of the act, the number of organizations with internal audit departments was dwindling. Thanks to the hoopla that went on with the likes of Enron, WorldCom, and so forth, and the act, that has changed.

What's more, the internal auditors now have teeth in many organizations where once they were sometimes ignored. Almost 43 percent of the survey respondents indicated a qualitative improvement in the internal audit reviews. Alas, an even greater number, 57 percent, reported no improvement. While this may be because the quality of the reviews was high prior to the act, we do not believe this was always the case.

BACKUP FOR CHECK REQUESTS

As some reading this could attest, the backup for check requests is sometimes less than ideal. In fact, in some organizations, no backup is required. This, of course, leads to duplicate payments and sometimes fraud. The lack of backup and documentation makes it difficult to determine what is being paid, if it was paid prior, and if it is appropriate.

With the passage of the act, a few organizations took a look at the documentation requirements for check requests and tightened things up. In fact, over 42 percent decided a check request with a signature and no backup really would not cut it anymore.

RECORDS RETENTION POLICY

Records retention is one of those areas that still remains largely ignored. In fact, even after the debacles that led to the passage of the Sarbanes-Oxley Act, most organizations have not tightened up their records retention policy. Almost three-quarters have not taken any serious action in this regard. And this is with regards to their payment information.

1099 REPORTING

For many organizations, their 1099 processes are a ticking bomb that will result in their paying big fines due to poor policies. Just a little over one-quarter of the survey respondents indicated they had improved their 1099 reporting processes.

The IRS takes this issue very seriously—so seriously that many expect corporate reporting to be required for services in the near future. Exactly when depends on the outcome of current political wranglings. This will be a disaster for all those organizations that take a lackadaisical approach to getting W-9s before making a payment. If you have a difficult time getting 1099s out in January now, when you have to issue them only to independent contractors, think what a disaster you will have on your hands when you have to issue them for every payment made for services.

While this is only tangentially a fraud concern, it will become a huge nightmare for those not currently

49

- Getting W-9s from every vendor and
- Checking the information using the IRS TIN Matching Program

before the first payment is made.

INVOICES

Invoice fraud, as discussed in Chapter 9, continues to be a serious concern. The proliferation of phony invoices has not abated. The use of electronic invoicing helps stem that problem. Just over one-quarter of the respondents to the survey indicated they moved to electronic invoicing as a result of concerns raised after the passage of the Sarbanes-Oxley Act, while over half said that the act did not have any material affect on their use of electronic invoicing.

Close to 15 percent believed that the act was not applicable to their decision to use (or not use) electronic invoicing.

When it comes to the way organizations process invoices, do the three-way match, and issue checks, just under 15 percent indicated that they changed the way they addressed these processes in reaction to the passage of the act. Clearly, most felt they had the processing issues under control and did not need to make any sort of radical change to conform with the new laws.

MASTER VENDOR FILE

As discussed in Chapter 10, the opportunity for internal fraud is ripe in those organizations that don't use proper controls surrounding the master vendor file. And too many organizations ignore the controls that should be used around this important repository of vendor information.

Yet, the act did not seem to make the point in this area. Just over 28 percent reported making any changes in their master vendor file controls. That means over 70 percent didn't see the writing on the wall, and a good number continue with master vendor file practices that would enable an internal fraudster looking for easy access.

OTHER REGULATORY CONCERNS

When it comes to issues related to accounts payable, sales and use tax along with unclaimed property are the regulatory issues that first come to mind, once 1099s and other information reporting issues are wiped from the plate.

The sad fact is this: According to the survey, few respondents took heed when Sarbanes-Oxley was enacted to improve their processes in these two important arenas. They continue largely ignored, although with stepped-up enforcement actions on the part of most of the states. This will no longer work in the next few years.

USING THE ACT TO ENFORCE NEEDED CHANGE

A number of the respondents shared their secrets on how they used the act to convince their bosses to make certain procedural changes. More than a few were forthright that the act gave them the tools they needed to convince upper management that improvements in their internal controls were needed. These managers also used the act to increase awareness in their staff, not only of internal controls but also government legislation.

I call it the Sarbanes-Oxley stick. Whenever management is resistant to a proposed change, savvy managers at organizations where it works start talking about violating Sarbanes-Oxley strictures. In some organizations, that's all it takes. In others, management demands more than some vague threats.

THE ACT AND ITS EFFECTS ON PRIVATE COMPANIES

Occasionally, professionals think they do not have to be concerned about the act because they do not work for a publicly traded company. This is a big mistake. Aside from the fact that conforming to the strictures of the act is likely to make your organization harder to defraud, there are more practical reasons for conforming. Specifically:

- Some banks are requiring compliance if they have a credit relationship. This may not be formal, but loose controls are something few lenders are willing to tolerate.
- Some customers are requiring that all key vendors be compliant.

And then there's the issue of its making good business sense.

ETHICS

The act requires a written code of ethics. This is an opportunity—yes, I do mean opportunity—for organizations everywhere #50 to let their employees, vendors, and customers know what is expected of them. It removes any doubt. It lets employees know exactly where the company stands when it comes to ethics and fraud. It also gives management the chance to set the right tone from the top. It lets them spell out what is expected in black and white, leaving nothing to interpretation.

WHISTLE-BLOWER PROTECTIONS

The act also enacted certain protections for whistle-blowers. Publicly held companies are now required to have a venue in place to receive the reports of anonymous whistle-blowers. Specifically, the act says "no publicly traded company, or any officer, employee, contractor, subcontractor, or agent of such company may discharge, demote, suspend, threaten, harass, or in any other manner discriminate against an employee in the terms and conditions of employment because of any lawful act done by the employee."

Retaliation against a whistle-blower is not only bad business, it is now also against the law. As discussed in Chapter 1, fraud is most frequently detected through an anonymous tip or by accident. This is an important consideration when encouraging whistle-blowers. Without them, many frauds would go undiscovered and continue to zap precious resources from the organization. That is just one reason why the whistle-blower protections are so important.

THE ANONYMOUS HOTLINE

Even with the protections promised by the law, many people are still reluctant to come forward. They do not really trust that the protections will stand up under the light of day, nor do they trust that word will not get back either to their boss or to the person they are blowing the whistle on. That is why hotlines are so important.

They also address the concerns of those employees who want to make management aware of the wrongdoings going on but do not wish to be involved in the ongoing investigation. An anonymous hotline provides them with a venue to alert management to something that is going on without becoming involved. Again, this can be crucial in uncovering a fraud that has been ongoing and would not come to light without a little nudge from someone with a little inside knowledge.

Now, some object to the anonymous features of these hotlines out of concern that false reports will occasionally be made. And this is a legitimate concern. That is why the charges made on the hotlines are not automatically assumed to be true and a careful investigation is undertaken before a charge is considered valid. This concern does not undermine the value of the hotline; it simply puts them into a certain perspective.

Whether an organization is public or private, hotlines, like suggestion boxes, are a good idea. Not everything that comes through them will be worth pursuing, but a lot of what does appear will be information that management would never have uncovered without the opportunity for someone to share it anonymously.

CONCLUDING THOUGHTS

Although at first glance it may appear that Sarbanes-Oxley has little to do with accounts payable, the initial reaction is not correct. In addition to the obvious areas, savvy professionals are getting behind the act to push for needed changes in all areas where internal controls are crucial.

Appendix A
FRAUD SCHEMES: PHYSICAL AND VIRTUAL CHECKS

Check fraud is a generic term representing a wide range of fraudulent schemes attributable to paper checks. The following are a few types.

- *Forgery.* This can either be a forged maker signature or a forged endorsement.
- *Counterfeiting.* Various methods are used to duplicate existing checks or fabricate new ones.
- *Alterations.* This generally refers to the use of household chemicals and solvents to remove or modify handwriting and information on a check.
- *Paperhanging.* Sometimes referred to as closed account fraud, paperhanging occurs when checks are written and/or reordered from an account that has already been closed.
- *Bust-out.* Also known as Regulation Z fraud, a bust-out scheme begins when a bad or fraudulent "booster" check is written to pay off a credit card balance. Since most banks credit the payment immediately, the cardholder's credit line is temporarily and artificially inflated. Goods and services are purchased before the check returns unpaid.
- *Kiting.* Kiting involves opening accounts at multiple locations and then moving fictitious funds between them.

- *Account compromise.* This involves a stolen account number.
- *Fictitious account.* A fictitious account is created by combining a legitimate account number with a noncorresponding routing and transit number. The check ends up being routed to the wrong fed district, thus creating float and allowing the perpetrator to remain undetected.

Appendix B

2007 TOP FRAUDS[*]

Note: Fake check scams top both fraud lists for the first time.

2007 Top Internet Frauds
1. Fake check scams
2. General merchandise
3. Auctions
4. Nigerian money offers
5. Lotteries
6. Advance fee loans/credit arrangers
7. Prizes/sweepstakes/free gifts
8. Phishing/spoofing
9. Sweetheart swindles
10. Internet access services

2007 Top Telemarketing Frauds
1. Fake check scams
2. Prizes/sweepstakes/free gifts
3. Advance fee loans/credit arrangers
4. Lotteries/lottery ticket buying clubs
5. Phishing/spoofing
6. Magazines

Source: National Consumers League.

7.   Credit card issuing
8.   Scholarships/educational grants
9.   Buyers clubs
10. Nigerian money offers

Appendix C
SEGREGATION OF DUTIES

When it comes to internal controls, much has been written about proper segregation of duties. The segregation is considered necessary as a fraud deterrent. Given the nature of accounts payable and the related functions, this is a crucial consideration. Following is a partial list of duties related to accounts payable and how they should be segregated.

The person responsible for bank reconciliation should not:
- Handle unclaimed property reporting.
- Be a signer on a bank account.

The person who is a check signer should not:
- Authorize invoices for payment on an account on which he/she is also a signer.
- Have ready access to the check stock.

A person who is responsible for the check stock should not:
- Be an authorized signer.
- Handle the bank reconciliations.
- Have access to the facsimile signer.

The person responsible for the facsimile signer should not:
- Have access to the check stock.

The person who is responsible for the master vendor file should not:
- Be an authorized signer.
- Be able to approve invoices for payment.
- Handle unclaimed property.

The person responsible for unclaimed property should not:
- Have responsibility for bank reconciliation.
- Have access to the master vendor file.

Individuals responsible for accounts payable functions should not also:
- Be responsible for accounts receivable.

Organizations with small accounts payable staffs may face some challenges when trying to coordinate an appropriate segregation of duties along with assigning backup responsibilities to handle absences and vacation. Sometimes it may be necessary to work with other departments to ensure the appropriate segregation of duties.

Appendix D

THE SARBANES-OXLEY ACT OF 2002
TITLES

The entire Act can be downloaded from http://frwebgate.access
.gpo.gov/cgi-bin/getdoc.cgi?dbname107_cong_reports&docid
f:hr610.107.pdf.

TITLE I—PUBLIC COMPANY ACCOUNTING OVERSIGHT BOARD

TITLE II—AUDITOR INDEPENDENCE

RESOURCES

Accounts Payable Books (published by John Wiley & Sons)
New Payment World: A Manager's Guide to Creating an Efficient Payment Process (2007)
Travel and Entertainment Best Practices (2007)
Controller and CFO's Guide to Accounts Payable (2006)
Accounts Payable & Sarbanes Oxley: Strengthening Your Internal Controls (2006)
Essentials of Accounts Payable (2002)
Accounts Payable Best Practices (2004)
Accounts Payable: A Guide to Running an Efficient Department (2004)

CRYSTALLUS, Inc.
Fee-based newsletter, *Accounts Payable Now & Tomorrow*
You can get a trial subscription at www.ap-now.com.
Free weekly e-zine, *e-AP News* (written by author)
You can sign up for it at www.ap-now.com/ezinesignup.html.
Accounts payable consulting and training: www.ap-now.com/consulting.html.
Accounts payable–related Webinars: www.ap-now.com/webinar.html.

Professional Fraud Detection and Prevention Associations
Association of Certified Fraud Examiners is the world's premier provider of antifraud training and education. Together with nearly 45,000 members, the ACFE is reducing business fraud worldwide and inspiring public confidence in the

integrity and objectivity within the profession. For additional information, go to www.acfe.com.

Association of Certified Fraud Specialists, Inc. is an educational, nonprofit corporation. For additional information, go to www.acfsnet.org.

National Association of Fraud Investigators was established to improve communications and to expand the networking of those in investigation and related fields, including but not limited to law enforcement officers, insurance investigators, professional investigators, security specialists, bond enforcement agents, attorneys, forensic examiners, tracers/ locators, credit card investigators, auto theft investigators, and international counterparts. For additional information, go to www.nafraud.com.

Pacific Northwest License, Tax & Fraud Association (PNLTFA) is an organization of public and private employees dedicated to the administration of enforcement of tax, license, and business registration laws, and the detection, investigation, prosecution, and prevention of fraud and fraud-related crimes. For additional information, go to www.pnltfa.com.

National Health Care Anti-Fraud Association is the leading national organization focused exclusively on the fight against health care fraud. For additional information, go to www.nhcaa.org.

Useful Links for Additional Fraud Information/Training

For phishing alerts: www.fraudwatchinternational.com/ phishing/index.php

For upcoming fraud Webinars offered by ACFE: http://eweb .acfe.com/eweb/DynamicPage.aspx?Site=ACFE&WebCode =AllSeminarevt

For fraud information from VISA: http://usa.visa.com/ merchants/risk_management/payment_card_fraud.html

For Preventing Payment Card Fraud white paper from the Philadelphia Fed: www.philadelphiafed.org/pcc/consumer/ fraud.pdf

For fraud article from Bottomline Technology: www.bottomline .com/news_events/newsletter/summer2005/article3.htm

For information about Apex Analytix's First Strike Technology: www.apexanalytix.com/Goods_and_Services/Continuous_ Monitoring/

For CD "How to Detect & Prevent T&E Fraud": www.shop.ap-now.com/product.sc?productId=143

For CD "Fraud in the Real World": www.shop.ap-now.com/ product.sc?categoryId=7&productId=137

INDEX